MEDIA ACCLAIM

How to Quit Churc

MW00640346

"Confronting hypocrisy, co........................ ....modern-day
Christianity head-on, Zender raises serious criticisms without renouncing
true faith. A truly fascinating book, and compelling reading for faithful
churchgoers and disillusioned church members alike."

Michael J. Carson
The Midwest Book Review

"Zender's book will no doubt cause great irritation to clergy members
everywhere. But it's only because no one has had the courage to state ideas
as critical as his."

Dan Julian
The State News

"Zender's conversational writing style turns discussion about strict religious dogma into a fun-filled frolic. Although vehemently spiritual, he is
the Robin Williams of the roadside tent revival. It is a provocative, intellectual romp through the Bible basics."

Dwight Greene
Fort Worth Star-Telegram

"Zender writes in such an informed, entertaining, and challenging way
that one experiences a whole series of epiphanies as they make their way
through this delightful look at how religion works in our lives."

Alan Caruba
Bookviews

"Reading Zender makes you laugh, gets you mad, and starts you to thinking. His snappy, in-your-face writing grabs you as he forcefully tackles
hypocrisy that masquerades as religion."

Chris Meehan
The Kalamazoo Gazette

"An excellent book that is part of what are probably the three best books
on the problems of the church today."

Harold McFarland
Readers Preference Reviews

WHAT READERS ARE SAYING:

How to Quit Church Without Quitting God

"This is simply one of the best books I've ever read. I laughed and cried throughout. Martin Zender humorously illustrates the limits of man's mind, while at the same time challenging believers to quit hanging their brains in the church foyer." —A.H.

"One time I was laughing so hard I had to remove my contacts. Next, I was crying. Then I realized, 'Wow, I'm being educated.' Blending spirituality with entertainment is an achievement few have managed." —C.W.

"I don't think I have ever finished reading a book so fast - it was almost impossible to put down. We quit the church a year ago, but never really felt comfortable about it. This book put every doubt to rest." —K.S.

"I'd rather hang out with God and be myself than work hard at performing for the religious crowd. What a relief this book is! If anyone else tries to shame me or hit me over the head with religious guilt, I will hit them over the head with this book!" —P.R.

"While visiting the library last week I came upon your book. The moment I opened it, I had to sit down. I had finally found someone who understood my feelings. With tears in my eyes, I read half the book right there in the library. I know I am just starting on this new way of thinking, but I feel free for the first time as a 'Christian'." —K.H.

"A ray of sunshine in the otherwise dark and dreary world of religious pomposity." —J.N.P.

"This book is like a tough cowboy with a soft heart." —R.F.

"Zender bands the readers together to resist religious exploitation. You will find yourself being pricked often, and even thinking Zender has gone too far. Then, suddenly, he resolves the conflict with a masterful touch. I don't think anyone can read this book without being emotionally and spiritually captivated." C.D.

"This book reads like an Alice in Wonderland adventure." —K.P.

About the Author

Martin Zender is known as The World's Most Outspoken Bible Scholar. He is an essayist, conference speaker, radio personality, humorist, and the author of several books on spiritual freedom. His essays have appeared in the *Chicago Tribune*, the *Atlanta Journal-Constitution*, the *Cleveland Plain Dealer*, and other newspapers. He has hosted the Grace Café radio program at WCCD in Cleveland, and the syndicated Zender/Sheridan Show at flagship station WBRI in Indianapolis. **www.martinzender.com**

Sheila Leeds

HOW TO QUIT CHURCH WITHOUT QUITTING GOD

Why going to church today is unbiblical, un-Christlike, and spiritually risky.

martin zender

HOW TO QUIT CHURCH WITHOUT QUITTING GOD

Why going to church today is unbiblical, un-Christlike, and spiritually risky.

Starke & Hartmann, Inc.

How to Quit Church Without Quitting God

© 2014 by Martin Zender

Second Edition, Paperback
First Edition, Hardcover © 2002 by Martin Zender

Published by Starke & Hartmann
P.O. Box 6473
Canton, OH 44706
www.starkehartmann.com
1-866-866-BOOK

Publisher's Cataloging-In-Publication Data
(Prepared by The Donohue Group, Inc.)

Zender, Martin.
    How to quit church without quitting God : why going to church today is
unbiblical, un-Christlike, and spiritually risky / Martin Zender. -- 2nd ed.

    p. : ill. ; cm.

    Issued also as an ebook.
    ISBN-13: 978-0-9842548-3-5 (pbk.)
    ISBN-10: 0-9842548-3-8 (pbk.)

    1. Church attendance. 2. Commitment to the church. 3. Christianity. 4.
Spirituality. I. Title.

BV4523 .Z46 2014
264   2013955619

To my sister Kelly

ABOUT THE SCRIPTURE TRANSLATIONS
USED IN THIS BOOK

Whenever I quote Scripture, accuracy is my first concern, but I also like paraphrased versions because of the relaxed language. I have struck a compromise. As long as the basic thought of the passage agrees with the more literal texts, I use J.B. Phillips' *The New Testament in Modern English.* (All verses without a reference are from Phillips.) But if Phillips blows it (and he often does) by sacrificing meaning for the sake of looser language, I quote from the *Concordant Literal New Testament.* When it comes to accuracy, this is my version of choice. It's the translation I have found to be most consistent in its uniform English renderings of Greek and Hebrew words. I quote from the *New American Standard Bible* once, though I'm not sure why. Whenever I need a more familiar frame of reference, I use the *King James Version* (KJV). But again, I do this only if the KJV happens to agree with the literal texts. I actually saw it happen once.

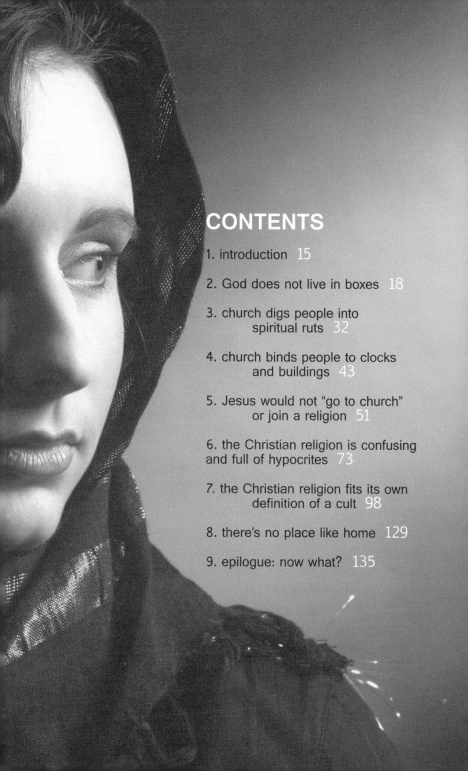

CONTENTS

"The God Who makes the world and all that is in it, He, the Lord inherent of heaven and earth, is not dwelling in temples made by hands."

—the apostle Paul
Acts 17:24
Concordant Literal New Testament

1.
INTRODUCTION

INTRODUCTION

Besides a riot, the title of this book will likely incite seven different reactions (seven being the number of perfection). The first non-rioting reaction will be: "Why would anyone *want* to quit church?" These folks will be so irritated by the title itself, and the mere suggestion that church could be expendable for the God-loving person, that they will not even pick up the book—unless no one is watching, of course. If no one is watching, they will page through it quickly, laugh to themselves at several of my cartoons, and then unhand it with a holy "Humph!"

The second group will say the same thing: "Why would anyone want to quit church?" But they will italicize the word "would." Like this: "Why *would* anyone want to quit church?" These folks come across as if they don't want to quit church, but they really do—and would—if they could justify it. The emphasis on "would" indicates, to me, that these people want answers. (Do I ever have answers.) Italic placement like this is a red carpet for a guy like me.

Church is not only expendable—it hinders spiritual growth.

The next group will say: "Why would *anyone* want to quit church?" This is big trouble. These people consider any and all persons outside the institutional box of religion to be stupid and/or dangerous. Unlike those in the first group, who merely unhanded the book with a holy "Humph!" these are militants—much like the Pharisees of Jesus' day—many of whom sport beards. They will march the book up to the bookseller and say, "How can you carry such a gross departure from the mainstream as this?" And the bookseller will say, "Because we just sold ten copies in the last hour." This will so infuriate the mainstream religious bearded person that he (or possibly, she) will place hell tracts in the restroom.

Yet another group will italicize the word "quit": "Why would anyone want to *quit* church?" These people are doers. They can't imagine relaxing. They define their life by service. They are Marthas, not Marys. Mary sat at the feet of the Lord and listened (Luke 10:38-42), while Martha fretted in the kitchen preparing the meal of the year. Jesus wasn't going to say anything until Martha thought her calling was the best. She said (I'm paraphrasing): "Tell my sister to get off her pretty little rear end and help me." Jesus said (again, paraphrasing): "You know, thanks for the epic meal, Martha—and for the apt description of Mary's posterior—but peanut butter sandwiches and pickles would have been fine. No one really needs frilly toothpicks. If you must know—since you brought it up—Mary is doing the better thing, and it won't be taken from her."

Doers hate this message (they ignore this passage of Scripture), because it teaches that sitting at the Master's feet is better than trying to impress Him. None of these people, then, will buy my book. To them, quitting church is "too easy." Quitting church is for people who are "just not serious" about "serving God." These people "just know" that serving and worshipping God should be anything but easy. It should be harder than doing one-hundred push-ups in the rain in a gorilla suit.

The next group will emphasize the word "to," like this: "Why would anyone want *to* quit church?" I don't understand these people at all, so let's move on to the next group.

This group will italicize the word "church," like this: "Why would anyone want to quit *church?*" Once again, I'm cooked—haven't got a chance here. These people love the building. Someone got to them, early on, with incense and peppermints. In other words, they got snowed by production. Maybe it was incense, maybe it was a carpeted altar, maybe it was a really good band with a hot-looking guitar player and a drummer with a soul patch. Maybe it was theater seating. It could very well have been the *size* of the church. Either it was so huge that the people thought, "God *has* to be here!" Or it was so small and quaint, that the people thought, "God *has* to be here!" Either way, they are in love with the building, the layout, the design, the furniture, and the smell. What do *I* have to offer against this? Only this: fellowship with God that exists always, no matter what the circumstance, no matter what condition the carpet, no matter what the lighting. (I should have mentioned lighting earlier. Lighting is so *very* important to people who emphasize the word, "church.")

Which brings us to the last group. Ah, the last group. They will not say a word as they experience a happy thrill deep down in their spirits. They will think to themselves, *I knew it.* Something about the cover, the title, and the little bits of text they pick up while paging through the book, will confirm things for them they have known, in their spirits, for a long, long time.

Welcome.

In a nutshell, this book describes the joy and freedom you will experience by quitting organized religion. By necessity, it must expose the world's most popular religion, and the hypocrisies that poison it. The way I see it, no one can properly enjoy God from the perspective of an institution. But who will quit the institution if they think everything is "just fine" there? But nothing is "just fine" there, not even close. So I sound the call to freedom. I do this, not by promoting my own authority or instructing you from my podium (the method of most "how-to" authors), but by pointing out the spiders on the institution walls and demonstrating how green (and pest-free) is the grass on the other side.

I believe one of the main reasons the world rejects Jesus Christ is that it thinks He's a member of the religion bearing His name. If only the world realized how much Jesus hates hypocrisy, ice-cream socials, and repetitive worship songs, they would depart without compunction. I saw a bumper sticker recently that said, "I have no problem with God, it's His fan club I can't stand."

Millions of church people today secretly want to quit church, but they balk because they think that if they quit church, they'll be quitting God. No. God and His Son quit organized religion years ago, and haven't been back. (Well, they never were members in the first place.) And would you believe me if I told you that not one person in the Bible ever "went to church"? The church is people, not an address on Main Street. One does not *go* to it, one *is* it.

Do you go to church every week? Then this book will challenge you. Have you walked away from organized religion? Then this book will comfort you. Have you avoided religion all your life? You may be a spiritual genius.

2.

GOD DOES NOT LIVE IN BOXES

GOD DOES NOT LIVE IN BOXES

According to recent news reports, spiritual seekers are forsaking religious institutions en masse. "A revival is under way," writes Stephanie Nolen of the *Toronto Globe*, "but for a phenomenon with Jesus at its center, it has surprisingly little to do with mainstream religion."

"People aren't really going back to church," says Professor Peter Emberley at Carleton University in Ottawa, in the same article. "They're circling on the edges."

Writing for the *New York Times*, Laurie Goodstein reports that "a growing number of Christians across the country are choosing a do-it-yourself worship experience." Goodstein labels it a "decentralized religious phenomenon." The cause? "Some are rebelling against the contemporary culture of the megachurch ... Others say they have been alienated by pastors who hoard power."

Jeffery L. Sheler of *U.S. News* offers this explanation: "We profess fidelity to traditional morality yet champion individual freedom and resist religious authoritarianism."

Speaking from the perspective of the trench rather than a news desk, I would explain the phenomenon with fewer syllables: We love God, but we don't need a church board telling us what to believe. We want honest answers to our biggest questions, but the organized church has been hedging on us and can't look us in the eye. We want a freelance walk with Jesus Christ, but the church has put Him in a box and said in so many words: "Worship *our* version of the Savior—or else."

There are reasons why the organized church acts this way, reasons that go far deeper than contemporary culture, power, and religious authoritarianism.

I have longed for God ever since becoming convinced that there was One. And yet, during thunderstorms and Mass, I wondered whether God longed for me in the same pleasant sense.

My parents loved me and wanted the best for me. They wanted me to have a religious education, so they sent me to Catholic school, and we all went to Catholic church.

My dad saw through all the pre-fabricated pomp and production, but went to church anyway for the sake of our family. He endured a lot of ritual in the Catholic church for many years, just to make my mother happy and give my sister Kelly and me a religious education. I honor my dad for that. My dad must have been related to Job, because of his patience and all the kneeling and standing he endured for our sakes. I was not as patient and only lasted a year after realizing that the Catholic church was built on the guilt of doing or not doing certain things for the distant

Deity. So maybe my dad wasn't related to Job after all (if he had been, then I'd be patient too), but God simply gave him this fruit of the spirit in spite of going to church.

I tried to be a good Catholic, mainly because I wouldn't get a cookie if I didn't. I went up and down like they told me to. I stood when I was supposed to stand; I knelt when I was supposed to kneel. I tried to sing the songs, but I couldn't sing and still can't. They weren't songs anyway—they were *hymns*. I thought at the time that the difference between a song and a hymn was sadness. Why was God always so sad? Why did He write songs to which no one could tap their foot? Dance to?

Light came through the stained glass of our church windows to make us all blue. The famous people in the glass allowed the passing light to turn them to frozen saints. The images were unnaturally warped, and inside the glass were little gas bubbles. What I wanted to know was: Where were the flesh and blood citizens of that ordinary world? Peter hauled fish; Paul made tents; Jesus walked with His disciples down dirt roads toward Jericho; they all spat. And why was not a single Bible person in these sad scenes drinking coffee?

If I had designed the church windows, my real-color saints would have big, heavy coffee mugs balanced on their knees, or cradled in their hands. Other, more active individuals, would be jogging down scraggly lanes with little backpacks, or frying eggs in a pan over a campfire. In my scenes, you would see kids brushing their teeth and dogs wagging their tails (not sure how I would depict the tails actually wagging, but I would try). Other people (adults and children alike) would be bending over double, laughing at a pun. Why not? Some onlookers (people who didn't get the pun) would just be standing there staring at the artist, like people do in photographs today.

I was sure that if Abraham or Moses or Peter or Paul came back and saw their warped, gas-bubbled likenesses in the glass at my church, they would throw rocks through the halos and scatter the startled congregants. "Run away from this place and *live!*" they would say. Peter would be flapping between the pews, rousing us from our stupor. We would see at once that the man flapping among us was certainly not the static saint of the pristine glass. "Where are your regular shoes?" Peter would ask a young lady next to me. "You can't run away from here in *those!*" And his coffee (in the glazed pottery mug in his left hand) would be spilling all over the place. Some of it would get on my pants. I would love every minute of it.

Peter was no hero, and neither was Paul. The "Bible heroes" were "Bible heroes" only because God took common folks and did amazing things through their sorry vessels.

Where was Jesus through all this? Eventually, I found out. Jesus was in heaven, sparkling with stars, planets, and some very fast comets. So why did my church stick Him on the cross above the altar and leave Him so lonely? I stared at that horrible crucifix through many a sad hymn. Why couldn't Jesus come down and lead us outside beneath a tree, or gather us in a meadow underneath the sun? Was I always supposed to think of Him as pierced and dead?

I take some of that back. In December, Jesus came off the cross long enough to crawl back into His cradle. But by January 1, He was back on the cross again. Guy Lombardo was be-bopping all over the place; men and women were dancing beneath revolving crystal; champagne was bubbling over onto pink opera gloves; and there was Jesus—hanging, dying, dripping blood before His weeping mother and the universe.

Cradle, cross, cradle, cross, Winter and Spring. Stand, kneel, sit. Why wouldn't they let Jesus be where He was? Why wouldn't they let us get up, walk the aisles, and mingle with each other? Even on jets at 30,000 feet, they let you get up and mingle.

I left the church because I eventually couldn't stand sitting there when I knew God was outside having a good time with the weather.

How did I leave the church? I was listening to a sermon one day, many years later, and it crashed headlong into what I was learning on my own about the real, living Jesus. If I remembered what the sermon was about, I would print it on the facing page so that you could tear out the page, tack it on a wall, and throw a pie at it. I'm not trying to be mysterious; I just can't remember it.

I was twenty years old.

I had already seen the movie *Jesus of Nazareth*, and so I'd already felt some deep pull from God that raised me out of the pew while everyone else was still stuck there. I had felt the depth of Jesus, had seen the sparkle of God, had begun to appreciate how all creation vibrated with God's life, even the apparently bad things. So I just leaned over and whispered to my mom, "I'm leaving."

And I walked out.

The sunshine blinded me, and air had never felt so rushing. My mom did ask me later in the car what was wrong, and I couldn't really explain it to her. I said, "I just feel different about everything." We never could approach the subject comfortably after that.

I should tell you more about that movie *Jesus of Nazareth*. It was April of 1979 when I first witnessed that production. The first part of the movie was phony, if you ask me. It was easy to sense that the director was sitting somewhere just off the soundstage. The hands of Jesus shook when He did miracles, which I doubt actually happened, because miracles, for Jesus, were easy. The re-enactment of the crucifixion in part two, however, was directed by God Himself, while every person on the soundstage must have sat there slack-jawed, or weeping.

Where did they find this Robert Powell guy who portrayed Jesus? What did they do to his eyes—or *were* those his eyes? They were so focused and pure and blue and tired from looking into the

sinew of every dull heart alive then. I watched Jesus drag His cross to the terrible hill. I had thought about that all my life, from the pew, and now I was seeing it enacted upon a screen. How I hated it! How could people do that? I hated everything about the blood and the cross. I wanted to turn away from such sorrows—but I couldn't.

A ridiculous car commercial came on after the crucifixion, which I couldn't bear to watch. The commercial must have ended, but I did not end. I had to go to my room so that everything could begin.

I went to my room and cried that open-mouth kind of cry that comes in spasms and doesn't quit until all your breath is gone. At that moment, and to this moment still, all I wanted was to learn what happened at that terrible hill outside Jerusalem. Who was the Person who would go through all that for me? He did it on purpose—on purpose! But *why* did He do it? Why did it have to happen to Him? So I said over and over again, "I have to know You, I have to know You, I have to know You." I said that phrase repeatedly through my tears.

It all came down to the cross, I knew that. As I said, I often stared at the crucifix above the altar at church. I'll say this for the Catholic church: It made me realize that something huge happened at the cross. The priests and nuns just never told me what it was. They themselves acted like nothing had happened there, because we all kept having to do stuff to purge ourselves of sin. But I couldn't imagine how any of my sin could possibly be left after what I had witnessed on the television.

As soon as I left the Catholic church, I knew I had to get a copy of Scripture. I had a feeling that all the information I needed was there. The Catholic church did not emphasize Bible reading. We all had to sit and stare at Father Passoli while *he* read the Bible. I even remember Father Passoli telling us one time not to follow along with him while he read. I couldn't figure out why he did that until years later. Then I finally realized that Passoli wanted everyone looking at him. He read very slowly and with great drama. Today, I feel it's a shame that he didn't have a skull to talk to, or a balcony to gaze up at.

(I'm now remembering the time Father Passoli had the marble in our church appraised. He published the results in the church bulletin, and Lord, we had some fine marble from somewhere in Italy. It was worth thousands or millions of dollars. Passoli wore a smile for three weeks that not even the deacons could wipe off. All the parishioners were supposed to be impressed by the marble. We were all supposed to walk with our heads a little higher, I guess, and feel sorry for all the churches that had crummy marble. All I remember is thinking, *So we've got nice marble. What has that got to do with anything? A lot of cemeteries have nice marble, too.*)

When I was younger, I thought the priests had it made. I thought, *who could possibly be closer to God*, because there were the priests doing all their work beneath the crucifix. I wanted very much to be close to God, so I envied the priests. Because apparently, Jesus Christ actually lived in a box on a little table next to the altar at our church.

There was a little gold box there, where the priests kept the bread for communion. The nuns used to tell us that Jesus lived in there, I mean, that He literally lived in there—in that box—and that He had his own appliances, furniture, guest room, etcetera. The nuns then asked for questions, so I raised my hand. I don't know why curtains were so important to me back then, but I asked if Jesus had curtains. I had to know. If Jesus had curtains, then that settled it—He lived there. One of the nuns—Sister Helen Therese—said, "Yes, of course Jesus has curtains."

So that settled it.

Martin Zender, good Catholic boy. 1966.

After leaving church, I started looking into Scripture—or maybe I did that before I left. I must have done it before, now that I think about it, because I had already learned some illuminating things about God, such as that He did not dwell in temples built by human hands (Acts 17:48), and that Jesus did not live in a gilded shoe box with curtains. I also learned all the things God *didn't* require of me.

The church told me I couldn't eat meat on Fridays during Lent. I always assumed this was in the Bible. It wasn't. There was nothing even close to that in the Bible. Naturally, this irritated me. In fact, the Bible said that people who were freakish about not eating meat on certain days were weak in faith, not strong (Romans 14:1-4). So what else was I taught that wasn't in the Bible?

Lots.

The church said I had to have my throat blessed regularly so I would never choke and die on a fish bone. I was told I had to stop eating chocolate for God during Lent, so I would know what Jesus went through on the cross. I was told to force myself every month to remember my sins and recite them to Father Passoli.

This part was awful. It was unbelievable pressure, shame, trial, and humiliation to tell somebody you didn't like all about your failings. Nobody could have made it more dramatic or spookier had they tried. The confessional had everything you needed to pee your pants: shadows, muted light, muted sound, walls surrounding you, stillness, a smell that suggested you were in the very presence of God. (I realize now that this was Old Spice, Father Passoli's favorite brand of aftershave.) Then, after I left the confessional, I had to go to a pew, kneel, and say whatever prayers Father Passoli told me to say. These prayers, along with the holy scent of Old Spice, were supposed to purge me of my sins.

Depending on how bad I was that month, I had to say ten Our Fathers, twenty Hail Marys, or some combination of the two. These two prayers were the heavyweights. Looking back, I can't believe I did these things. Saying prayers over and over to purge yourself of sin mocked what Jesus did on the cross. I did it, however, because they told me it was essential for salvation. What a revelation when I learned that Jesus took away all my sins: I never had to feel guilty again, not every month, not ever. It was deliverance. I felt the deliverance in the parable of the

"Hold still. Henry. This new prayer pill is worth ten Our Fathers."

wind that hit my face and spirit that day I left the church, and in the stone steps I descended for the final time to see cars whisking down the highway with glints of sunlight on their roofs and happy people inside going somewhere enjoyable.

I have to tell you about Eli Beachy, who used to be in a strange and very tight religion known as the Worldwide Church of God. God has since delivered Eli from the worldwide church of constant guilt, but listen to this.

One day, Eli and I were swapping stories of religious bondage. He told me how, on the Friday evening before "The Feast of Unleavened Bread," just after the Jewish feast of Passover, he and his wife had to empty their house of anything that might contain leaven. This was an Israelite rite from way back, instituted in the days before God gave clearer revelations of Himself through Jesus Christ. Why Eli had to worry about leaven twenty centuries after Christ, no one knew except Herbert Armstrong, the world leader of the church.

Eli ran a transmission business, so he often had several cars of customers parked at his place on weekends. So on that special Friday night, Eli had to go through every one of those cars with a DustBuster and sweep up any bread crumbs that might be in the cars. Why? Because the bread crumbs would have leaven in them. How amazing was that? That was heavyweight bondage. I shook my head. What a religious exercise driven by guilt to try to please God in an old, decrepit way that He doesn't care about any more.

Eli whipped *my* story. All I did was kiss a statue. I had to line up with the rest of the congregants on Good Friday, approach a priest holding a yardstick-sized crucifix, and kiss the bloody (red paint) feet of a plastic Jesus. So I was only an icon venerator. How that paled against being a bread crumb sweeper. There was no comparison. The only thing worse would be if Eli had to kiss the DustBuster—which he didn't.

The worst thing anyone can do is put God in a box. "Regular" Christians bash the Catholic Christians, but they shouldn't because they're guilty of the same thing. God is boxed, either way. One box may be bigger than the next; maybe there's a different label on the top of each box, or the box is another color. But all the boxes are factory-folded cardboard, sealed with the particular tape of the particular institution that made the box. There's nutrition information on the side, with a lot of "0%" showing up in every category.

There is a spiritual revolution in this country. Many magazines and newspapers are reporting it. People are fidgety, and they're leaving the institutional churches. This is a good thing. Factories make fine Twinkies, but no assembly line can produce people of God. Baptist seminaries produce Baptists, and Methodists seminaries produce Methodists. How does one produce a man or woman of God? It is the exclusive work of God's spirit. It happens without doors, deans, or diplomas. People are realizing this, so they're leaving the institutions to find truth.

Jesus is walking the shores again, and He's wandering up those hills rising so distantly from the temple. People are leaving church to find Him. As for the clergy, they're shoring up their crumbling structures with new drums, louder guitars, and the occasional chain-saw juggler. None of it works, so they lay new carpet. The pastors and priests think they're fighting some terrible withdrawal from faith. What the pastors and priests fail to realize is that *they* are the terrible withdrawal from faith.

People are smart, they always have been. The clergy don't seem to realize this.

Jesus Christ would never be a Christian. Christianity today has become a social club, and the glorified Christ is not so exclusive. This is one of the best reasons to leave church—that Jesus Christ is not a Christian. I'll say more on this later.

What all this means is that you can leave the institution without leaving Jesus. You can talk to Him or about Him in your home or at the office, with coffee, tea, beer; with friends, without sad organ music; and without getting up early on your only day off, all of which beats the heck out of the institutions. I can even show you in Scripture where people forsook status-quo religion and thrived. Many are names you will know: Abraham, Jesus, Peter, Paul. You probably already know that the people in the Bible who stayed institutionalized suffered from chronic bad moods and killed happy people.

I do thank my parents for doing what they thought was best for me by sending me to Catholic school and church. God is in charge of this world and no one can escape what He ultimately wants. My twenty years of Catholic experience gave me a thorough knowledge of religious bondage.

Without that, I would not appreciate how good it feels to be free.

3.
CHURCH DIGS PEOPLE INTO SPIRITUAL RUTS

CHURCH DIGS PEOPLE INTO SPIRITUAL RUTS

When I finally started reading the Scriptures on my own—as I've said—I found a lot there that nobody ever told me. For instance, when the apostle Paul was in Athens, he spoke to some superstitious philosophers who prayed to stone. Part of what Paul said was:

> God who made the world and all that is in it, being Lord of both Heaven and earth, does not live in man-made temples, nor is He ministered to by human hands, as though He had need of anything—seeing that He is the one who gives to all humans life and breath and everything else ... Indeed, it is in Him that we live and move and have our being.
>
> —*the apostle Paul*, to Athenian philosophers on Mars' Hill, Acts 17:24–25, 28

So God does not live in man-made temples. Why didn't anyone ever tell me that? Wouldn't that have been helpful information for me to have? It would have kept me from asking stupid questions about Jesus' curtains.

Appreciate how big Paul's "we" was when he said, "In Him *we* live and move and have our being." Paul put himself in the same boat as the rock worshippers. To Paul, he and the rock worshippers were all part of a common humanity. Paul for sure meant all humanity there, and not just believers. A Christian addressing the Athenian philosophers that day might have said:

"In Him, me and the others in my church live and move and have our being. And if you limestone-lickers would just go to *our* church, then maybe *you* could live and move and be in God, too."

But God does not live in man-made temples.

Some people don't know this yet (that God does not live in man-made temples) and so they continue to run in and out of their bedrooms and fidget with their hair while looking at their watches and yelling, "Come on! You kids get in the car right now! It's time to go worship God!" Just as many people in this world do not yet realize their common part in God, many believers do not yet know the joys of clock-free fellowship.

Or church in the quietness of everyday moments.

Jesus talked to a woman one day at a well in Samaria. This lady was worried about where to talk to God. Many people today have the same worry. She said, "Our ancestors worshipped on this hill-side, but you Jews say that Jerusalem is the place where people ought to worship" (John 4:20).

Jesus shook His head. He looked the woman in the eye and uttered a profound thing. "Believe me," He answered, "The time is coming when worshipping the Father will not be a matter of 'on

"Get in the car right now!"

this hill-side' or 'in Jerusalem.' The time is coming, yes, and has already come, when true worshippers will worship the Father in spirit and in reality" (John 4:21, 23).

Spirit and reality. It sure transcends "the corner of Broad and Ninth."

You want spirit and reality, yet many of your Christian friends seem only to want to stiffen their hair, hug people, eat chocolate chip cookies, sing songs, and go home.

Some people are stuck in the middle, and this is where I may be of assistance. Wherever you find tons of people gathered with

cookies and hairspray, you will not find truth. Truth tramps snow
at the tops of mountains. Truth contemplates incoming waves
on the island of exile. Truth is found alone in your bedroom, or
beneath trees. Truth is two people walking down the road heart-
to-heart. Their hair may be nice, but they don't really care at the
moment.

Truth is at the well, where you can also get a drink.

Some people have said to you, "You are not spiritual." I
know they have said this, because they're still saying it to me. But
remember, they are measuring your spirituality by their standard.
Their standard of spirituality is: "If you don't go to our church,
or follow our pastor, or if you are not baptized into our particular
club, then you are not spiritual."

As if they own the franchise on God. But this is why they are
so accusing, because they *think* they own the franchise.

But if you even think about God, then you are spiritual; or
if you lay awake wondering about The Big Picture in your bed
at night, then you are spiritual; or if you thank God for your
children, or even cry out in frustration at your life and let the
words fly into heaven, then you are spiritual.

I'm serious about the flying words; I did say that your words
were flying into *heaven.* At least you're addressing the Source of
Everything. This is what Job did. When his trials came, Job said, "I
am disgusted with my soul, and will give vent to my complaint!"
(Job 10:1). Concerning this outburst and other things Job said,
God later said: "Job has spoken of Me what is right" (Job 42:7).

God likes ragged honesty more than careful or formal
courtesy. I have arrived at this conclusion by experience. When
I am under great stress in my work, or am mourning death, or
have just heard of a tragic accident, or when the ordinary, daily
evils of this world gang up and overwhelm me, I cry to heaven

using words not ordinarily associated with people imploring the Deity. I have tried over the years to upgrade my stress-induced vocabulary; it hasn't worked. I have waited for God to do it; He doesn't see the rush. So away I go. After these tirades, when I have expected a lightning bolt, God has placed a hand gently on my shoulder instead, pulling me toward Him. I have found a deeper relationship with God through honesty than through any misguided attempts at piety. I have concluded from this that God likes it when people are real with Him and don't play games. I believe it may be a relief to Him from all the whispery, tippy-toe stuff He usually gets. The way I see it, if you can't tell your Maker what's happening to you, who can you tell? This takes spiritual maturity.

People who look beyond themselves for something bigger are spiritual people. People who will not be satisfied until they find the true God are spiritual people.

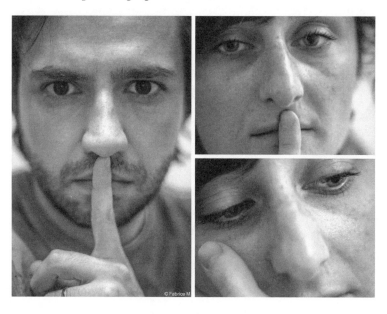

But it gets even better.

If you see through religious hypocrisy, then you are more spiritual than those people who do not see through it. If you have looked at the circus that the Christian religion has become, and thought: *Something is definitely not right about all this*, then you are more spiritual than those who have joined that religion and throw confetti at it, even though you can't quite put your finger on what's wrong with it.

You will see what's wrong with it. You have sensed something rotten in Pew-land, and you have been right all along. By the end of this book, you will know just how right you are.

I know there are many people reading who have somehow avoided equating truth with "institution." That's good, but there are others who think that they can't have truth *without* an institution. That's bad. In fact, truth requires that there be no walls or human regulations, which would (and do) choke the life from it.

The challenge is to not believe you're discarding Christ when you throw out the pipe organ. Many people think: *It's either the institution or a life without Jesus. I can't leave church and still have Christ.* I have good news for you: You have more hope of finding the real Jesus outside the institution than in it. It's just like it was when Jesus walked this earth. Where did He find true fellowship? He found it outside the walls of the temple. The best moments for Christ were on mountaintops and next to the sea, speaking with the so-called "low-life" among humanity. When it was time for Him to die, *then* He went back to the temple.

Besides, who are they worshipping there today in the institution? I know they say, "We're worshipping Jesus," but is it the real Jesus they're worshipping? Or is it a caricature of Jesus, painted with the particular brushstrokes of the institution? I know they're getting very excited and out-of-breath about *something*, I'm just wondering what it is. I know they say, "It's Jesus." Perhaps so, but they act the same way at football games.

Tonight it's football, tomorrow it's Jesus. It makes me wonder if excitement is the goal, rather than Jesus. For many, Jesus is the way to a fuller, more well-rounded *me*. The crosses around the neck suggest a hip religiosity, as if to say, "Jesus is my *thing*."

Look around you at the T-shirts, posters, and Jesus jewelry; the carpenter from Nazareth is very, very cool today. This should be a red flag that something is very, very wrong.

There is the false and there is the true. Speaking to the spiritual seeker, I understand you wanting nothing to do with the false. The tricky part is that the false and the true both use the same names. Both say "God," and both say "Jesus Christ." But does it mean that both are worshipping the same Beings? No. The false are worshipping the pop-icon "God" and "Christ," while the true are worshipping the real God and Christ. Or at least they are seeking the Real and will not be satisfied until they find Him.

What will you lose by fleeing the man-made walls? The truth? Just as trees do not grow in alleys, truth does not live between man-made walls. Truth abides in the heart. If the truth is in your heart, you can't lose it; truth is not so fragile. If it's something besides truth there, you don't want that anyway. It will blow away in your wake as you walk out the door.

Walls come and go, but truth endures. You can run and jump and live your happy life without worrying about losing truth—the *real* truth. This is not like the "truth" you had in the institution. That "truth" used to wait around to see what you would do with it, to see if you were worthy of it or could live up to its standards. And then, based on your behavior, it would adjust its opinion of you. It could damn you as easily as bless you, scare you as easily as comfort you. It all depended on—*you*.

Real truth is not like that. It's stronger and more sure of itself. Human foibles cannot hope to alter it.

So, when you are far from the noise and the crowds, take out the truth that remains in your heart. Withdraw the real thing and look at it. Turn it every which way. Turn it in the shade and in the sun. Examine it with a magnifying glass. Toss it in your dryer at home and tumble it on "hot." Truth will survive your every scrutiny because it has nothing to hide. No amount of rough treatment can diminish it; it is truth. Realizing this will cause you to relax for perhaps the first time in your life. In such a reclining position, you can now enjoy the truth in whatever new framework you choose. Serenade it with whatever new music you want in whatever new environment. It is now yours and it will never leave you.

I've just been realizing—as I've been writing—that there are probably more people than I realize who go to church mainly for social reasons. They probably think that the title of this book is stupid. They point it out to their friends and say, "Why would anyone *want* to quit church?" (I analyzed these people and their particular brand of italic placement in the Introduction.)

We are social creatures, it's true, but do we have to compromise spiritual integrity for the sake of it? We can play horseshoes together and go to movies together and climb mountains together without compromising spiritual integrity. Isn't this enough? Just how desperate are we to fix up our hair and "go someplace"?

It takes spiritual sensitivity to detect the absence of truth in the religious institution. This sensitivity is a rare, God-given gift. Without this gift, the music and the excitement of the pop-worship experience easily keep people from thinking: *Um, there seems to be something missing here.*

"Fun, food, and fellowship. I just can't take it any more, Pastor Dave.."

The masses are satisfied with status-quo spirituality (which is often only something that *looks* spiritual), as long as they can hobnob with their friends. If it goes with the flow, count them in. If it gets too deep or serious, or it makes them look weird, forget it.

"Fun, food, and fellowship" is the new holy trinity. And yet somehow, I cannot imagine that Peter, James, and John, when invited by Jesus to accompany Him to the Garden of Gethsemane, asked, "Will there be any attractive women there?"

Consider some Bible people who thrived in a freelance relationship with God. Abraham was one of them. This man was living in the homey little Bible town of Charan when God said to him, "Go from your land and from your father's house to the land which I shall show you" (Genesis 12:1).

Abraham never saw a pew again for the rest of his life.

God called Abraham from what he had always known and put him in a tent. Maybe God is doing that with you now. God may be calling you now from *your* father's house. I don't mean your literal house. I'm talking about the religion that has contained and defined you since childhood. The religion of your forefathers may be squashing your spirit. Abraham had the same problem. God tapped his longing and called him from status-quo-nothing-new into fresh-territory-every-day. (This is a regular thing in the Bible; it happens all the time.)

Abraham and his family were on the move through some serious desert after that, but desert isn't so bad; I've been there. I bicycled through the Mojave Desert on my way pedaling across the United States. Desert is clean and pure; the sun shines; you don't need lots of clothing; the traffic is light. Besides, there is the occasional oasis (otherwise known as a "Circle K" store) stuffed with chocolate chip cookies and cold milk. In his wanderings, Abraham never starved or evaporated. The God Who called him, took care of him. Abraham's eyes rested on stars, ferns, his wife, and kids, but never again on steeples, statuary, ushers, or parking lots.

Where was Abraham's country after that? He didn't have one. Truth is always that way. It travels in a tent through the desert. Do not fear tents. Did you know that your body, itself, is a kind of tent? It is a temporary tabernacle, moving you through this strange, hard life. Some tents are quite nice and cost a lot of money. Abraham was a rich man and had a *very* nice tent—I believe—filled with pillows, blankets, veils, and probably several foldaway cots.

This, however, is the fear some people have: They're afraid they'll get stuck with a crummy tent. They're afraid that if they leave the institution, they'll fall apart morally and spiritually. They'll leave church on Sunday and begin their life of crime on Monday. The organized structure comforts them because of the safety net of other people. Maybe the religious icons do them good: *If I keep looking at that poster of Jesus,* they think, *maybe I'll finally be like Him.* Or, *If I don't see that white dove in the painting above the altar every week, I might start gorging on cheesecake.*

This is when people have to follow their God-given instincts and trust Him. That's exactly what Abraham did. Abraham had no idea where he was going, no idea where God was leading him. All He knew was that God was calling him to a freelance relationship that didn't stay in any one place too long. Here is what the Scripture account says about Abraham:

> It was by faith that Abraham obeyed the summons to go
> out to a place which he would eventually possess, and he
> set out in complete ignorance of his destination. It was
> faith that kept him journeying like a foreigner through the
> land of promise, with no more home than the tents which
> he shared with Isaac and Jacob, co-heirs with him of the
> promise. For Abraham's eyes were looking forward to that
> city with solid foundations of which God Himself is both
> architect and builder. —Hebrews 11:8-10

I told you that I bicycled through the Mojave Desert. Yes. I had to cross that expanse on my way from Los Angeles to Boston. This was my transcontinental bicycle adventure of 1980. Briefly, it came about like this:

I told myself when I started college that if I wasn't happy with school after six months, I would do something about it. It isn't that I planned to be miserable by then, but that I would never settle for mediocrity. Ruts were not an option for me.

A weird thing happened then. I started school in September, and by the following February, I knew I was a stranger in a strange land. It hit me that I had escaped one system (high school), only to join another. People say you go to college to find out what you want in life. I didn't know these "people," so I decided to skip college and jump right into life.

On a cold day in February, my roommate came in to find me drinking chocolate milk and smiling like a monkey.

"What's up?" he said.

"That's it," I said. "I'm busting out of here."

He knew what I meant. "You're *quitting*," he said.

"I'm *starting*. I'm going to bicycle across the United States. Ramble around the country without an alarm clock. No time to wake up, no time to go to bed..."

"No money," he said. My roommate was always practical that way.

"I'll sell all these ridiculous anatomy books; who cares what the tendons that hold our ankles together are called? I'll sell this beanbag chair."

"What will you sit on when you get back?" he asked.

"I'll worry about that later," I said.

He then wanted to know if I'd talked to God about it; he was a Christian.

"Yes, I have. I think I should go because I feel peace about this. I'm going with my gut."

"Don't forget God," reminded my roommate.

"God invented my gut," I said.

I sold my anatomy books; my yellow beanbag chair brought five dollars. I worked at a restaurant until June, cooking eggs every morning at 6 a.m., to my patrons' specifications. As my days there waned, I bought packs, a tent, and a very light, green sleeping bag stuffed with the feathers of geese. I then went to the airport, and bought a one-way ticket to Los Angeles.

That summer lives forever. Los Angeles to Boston will never leave my life. I thank God, continually, for that summer.

Fruit waited in stands for me, where I never would have expected it, just when I needed a peach. Trees waited in roadside parks for me to sit under them. People waited their entire lives to invite me in for a cold drink. (That's how it seemed to me, anyway, because of how eager total strangers were to help me.) New roads came every day for forty-six days, so that I could continue my journey. God's arrangements were so plain to me as they sprang fresh from rocky crevasses and strangely named places.

Before I was born, God made the Mojave Desert, just for me. This is how I see it now. This desert was not in Ohio, so I had to leave my home state to find it. God kept the Rockies for me, and the Continental Divide at the proper slope, so that I could feel the earth move beneath me. The day finally came when He called me to see and feel these things. Valleys filled with fog feel cool when you crawl from your tent on a rainy July morning in Ogallala, Nebraska, even while the sun shines somewhere just below the horizon.

I never knew this before.

God, I lived. I lived and loved my life. Breakfast was from McDonalds, or sometimes from a fruit stand, or sometimes at the homes of people named Bill, Wilma, or Dutch and Rita Garland. Lunch got poured from a can of Pringles, supper—*who knows where?* I read Scripture by candle-lantern in my tent at midnight.

A tent in a rainstorm is a wonderful thing. Rain so close but it can't reach you—its fury frustrated by this marvelous sheath of nylon, provided you by God and a camping outlet. The candle-lantern displaces such a small piece of the night, and a micron of nylon keeps you from such watery misery that being warm and cozy so near these opposites makes you laugh. And sleep like a baby.

It was July 20, 1980, when I pedaled into Boston, Massachusetts in a misting rain, 3,364 miles removed from the person I had been. I had bicycled one-hundred miles that day, all the way from my campsite in a cornfield near Pittsfield. That distance would have intimidated me a month earlier, but on this day, the last day of my trip, it was nothing.

The sun was low when I made the ocean next morning, and it set everything to glowing. The thrill of seeing that water, after forty-six days of continuously moving toward it, turned me to a child again. I gave my camera to a bystander and asked him to snap a photo. The trip needed an exclamation point. Gathering

Mojave Desert.
Old Route 66.
Amboy, CA June 12, 1980.
5 days out of Los Angeles.

Entering Boston.
U.S. Route 20.
July 20, 1980.
Day 46.

my youthful exuberance, I leaped into the air. A moment before I returned to Earth, the stranger-turned-friend exposed the film. And so, thanks to this person I have never seen again, there is record of a man floating above Earth, content without a home, rejoicing on the edge of God's universe.

This is how to live.

I rode the unknown stripe. I found a depth in God that I never knew existed. What if I had never gone? I would be so poor right now. I shudder to think if I had never gone.

If God is calling you to go somewhere, then go. Don't wait. The unknown is not as frightening as you think. God is there now, setting everything up. Take that step and see what He has for you.

It seems right to talk now about Moses.

In Egypt as a young man in the palace of Pharaoh, Moses had it made. But then he found out he was an Israelite. Therefore, it was *his* people who were the slaves of Pharaoh. This troubled Moses' spirit. Moses had started life on a big river moving swiftly in a basket launched by the hands of his Israelite mother, and now he was stuck in a big cold palace watching his people grovel in bondage.

Moses broke down one day when he saw an Egyptian beating an Israelite. Moses killed the Egyptian with his bare hands. This was not a good thing, so Moses fled to the wilderness. What is it with this wilderness? It's a good place for sorting things out, that's what. Moses learned important things in the absence of hassle. Tending sheep gives a man time to think. Everything Moses did after that was tent-like, wide open to the discovery of new horizons.

Who ever heard of a burning bush? Nobody had seen anything like it. It was a new thing, for sure. Why not answer the bush and see what it has to say? Moses wouldn't have done that forty years before. He was too smart for it then. He had to be humbled to be able to talk to shrubbery.

When he returned to Egypt, Moses was a hillbilly in front of Pharaoh, a fool before the Egyptian courtiers—at first. He counted on God for every ridiculous word that came from his mouth, words like, "Let my people go" and "If I were you, I would hearken to these seemingly incoherent ramblings of mine." When Moses led the people from Egypt, out came the tents again. What is it with these tents? Truth is always moving, that's what. You camp for only so long, then you move. Truth is that way. It never digs a basement. As soon as it digs one, up comes an institution.

Ten years ago, I visited a super-active, big-city church. I think the church used to be a blimp hangar, it was that big. The church had its own band, its own printing press, and its own sun, I think. It seemed that planets revolved around it. There was even a football team: The Last Supper Lions. Everything was exciting at the church. The goal of the church was to spread as much of this excitement to as many people as possible by means of the printed word, face-to-face evangelism, music, solar flares, third-down conversions—and blimp ropes tied around the ankles (more about this bondage aspect soon).

The man who invited me to the church was in charge of the church's printing press. As far as I could tell, he was god of the printing press. His wife had a visible halo that disrupted cell phone operation. I am only half-joking about these things. Everything was hopping at the church the whole time I was there. There was a preaching service, a band concert, an abortion protest, and a new leaflet on Hell coming off the press, titled: *Pretty Much God Damn Those Who Don't Attend Our Megachurch.*

But I lived many miles from the holy megachurch/blimp hangar, and could not regularly attend, not that I would have. I lived in the country then, next to a dairy farm that was not at all holy. So it became time for me to leave. The megacouple said they would visit me soon at my outpost. Was I ever surprised when they did.

I thought they had come for a casual visit; I have always been just a tad naive. The couple was on a mission. Their mission was to ask us: *Where is your ministry?*

The man was tying a blimp rope around my right ankle when he looked up at me and asked, "Where is your ministry, fella? You're not serving the Lord."

I will never forget the man's wife looking out the window. She was looking across the road to a pasture. The pasture must have looked so peaceful to her. Then she said softly, yet loud enough for me to hear: "Yes, I can understand why people would want to live out here if they weren't interested in serving the Lord."

As soon as she said that, I thought about Moses. I thought about Moses tending sheep for forty years in the wilderness, being prepared in peace and quiet for a bush that would burn but not be consumed.

In A.D. 29, you did not join Jesus Christ by signing a statement of faith. You did not go to Jesus Christ's church, because it didn't have a settled location. What you did was you started following Him down the road. You walked beside the Man. On the way to Bethel, you heard things you didn't hear in the temple. You heard things like, "Watch what happens to this storm"; "Anybody have any fish?"; and "You've been right all along about your religious leaders in Jerusalem, because they *are* snakes and hypocrites."

The people who walked with Jesus loved this kind of thing. These were the kinds of people who are called lost and damned today by the people on Christian television. Religious leaders of every era look down at sinners. Only the noses have changed.

In Jesus' day, people who wanted truth came outside Jerusalem, to the hillsides and the fishing wharves—or to the bars, or to the "bad" side of town where the prostitutes lived. This is where the action was; I speak of truth. Truth was here because the people here were real. Their crime was that they distrusted the religious establishment. They could smell hypocrisy ten cubits away. They didn't fall for the temple paint job because they knew

"They were talking about us again today on Christian television."

what was behind it. They also knew the Real Deal when they saw it. Jesus came here with delight to watch His word take root inside these people. Because here, no religious leader got in the way to dam (or damn) the flow of truth.

> Later, as Jesus was in a house sitting at the dinner-table, many tax-collectors and other disreputable people came and joined Him and His disciples. The Pharisees noticed this and said to the disciples, "Why does your master have His meals with tax-collectors and sinners?"
> —Matthew 9:10–11

My paraphrase would read:

> Jesus came to the house of a redneck named Rod. In came a famous singer, four smokers, three women wearing belly-button rings, and an IRS agent. Jesus lounged with them, understood their problems, answered their questions, ate their pretzels. Pastor Bob heard about it later and asked Jesus' followers, "Excuse me, but um ... why does your guru eat pretzels with Lady Gaga?"

4

CHURCH BINDS PEOPLE TO CLOCKS AND BUILDINGS

CHURCH BINDS PEOPLE TO CLOCKS AND BUILDINGS

Why is everybody so anxious for me to go to church? If one more person quotes Hebrews 10:25 to me: "𝔇𝔬 𝔫𝔬𝔱 𝔣𝔬𝔯𝔰𝔞𝔨𝔢 𝔱𝔥𝔢 𝔞𝔰𝔰𝔢𝔪𝔟𝔩𝔦𝔫𝔤 𝔬𝔣 𝔶𝔬𝔲𝔯𝔰𝔢𝔩𝔳𝔢𝔰 𝔱𝔬𝔤𝔢𝔱𝔥𝔢𝔯" (and especially if they talk in this kind of font), I will try to be nice. But it won't work, I already know that. Because the person will notice a sudden change in my mood. This change will make them wonder to themselves, *Does Martin still like me?* This is because I will have become silent and moody and dark. I always become this way whenever people quote Scriptures to me that have nothing to do with what they think and wish and hope the Scriptures have to do with.

These troublesome people are talking about Hebrews 10:24–25: "And let us consider one another to provoke unto love and to good works: not forsaking the assembling of ourselves together, as the manner of some is ..." (KJV).

The verse is shaved of detail. Bald. Totally lacking hair. Yet, here is what the Scripture-quoters pack into the verse in their creative little minds: "Not forsaking the assembling of ourselves together by the dozens in church buildings every Sunday, as is the manner of Martin Zender, who hasn't been to church in thirty-two years."

Maybe something is wrong with my eyes. Where does the verse say any of that? Where does the verse say how often I'm supposed to assemble? Where does it say where I'm supposed to assemble? Where does it say who I'm supposed to assemble with? Where does it say how many I'm supposed to assemble with? Where am I, personally, being harassed by the writer of Hebrews? (Not to mention the book of Hebrews was written to Israelites—not Gentiles.)

Two can play this packing game. I can pack between the lines with as much boldness as the next packer, and offer the following as evidence of it: "Not forsaking the assembling of ourselves together once every five years beneath an evergreen tree with one other person and God, Who made the tree and has deemed this a fine place to discuss Abraham."

Yet this verse is an anvil over the heads of people who don't go to church.

We are going to a short Bible study now, thanks for coming. I don't know if you're used to this kind of thing, but it won't be like you think. It's not the kind of Bible study where people try to build higher fences around their little club. It's the kind of Bible study that will get these types of people off your back and give you the thrill of being able to use their own weapon against them. It's the kind of Bible study that will demolish fences and make you thankful you attended because of how it will let you sleep in on Sunday and drink orange juice on the sofa with your kids all morning and thank God that you have the day off and do not feel the least bit guilty about not having to rush off somewhere to "honor the Deity."

I am about to show you in Scripture how the word "church," by itself, has nothing to do with meeting once a week with the same old people in the same old building on Main Street. This will empower you, I promise. Scriptural evidence verifying all your hunches about what church *really* is will fill you with new power and purpose.

If you want to mess up your kids, say "yummy" while scraping dog poop off your shoe. From that day on, your kids will associate "yummy" with terrible smells like dog poop and sauerkraut. They absolutely won't know any better. People who say "yummy" while eating ice cream will puzzle your children for the rest of their sorry lives. Your children will say, "Those people are *weird*." But really, *your* kids are the weird ones because you messed them up with clashing words and contexts.

Context is that powerful.

Context is extremely important when you don't know a language. An unknown word in a known context defines the word. This principle especially works in Scripture. If you're not sure what a word meant to the people who wrote the word, you just go to some contexts where the people used that word. For instance, if they put the word *scchaffa!* in the mouths of people falling off camels and craggy precipices, be assured that *scchaffa!* answers somewhat to our *aaarghhh!*

I'm about to show you a context in Scripture where the word "church" appears. This context will show you how loose and spontaneous "church" really can be.

In the nineteenth chapter of the book of Acts, the apostle Paul is in the city of Ephesus on the west coast of Asia Minor. Ephesus was the headquarters of the goddess Diana. Diana was a flexible goddess, as far as her charms went. She borrowed her charms from an Asiatic fertility goddess and a Canaanite deity, Ashtoreth. Ashtoreth was the patroness of sexual instinct. Put these two goddesses together and you got a fairly good-looking statue with about forty-nine breasts.

There was a big shot silversmith in Ephesus named Demetrius who made lots of money selling statues of Diana. You can imagine the man's agitation when Paul comes to town telling people that "gods made by human hands are not gods at all" (verse 26).

Demetrius quickly starts a riot among his fellow silversmiths. He tells them, "Paul has succeeded in changing the minds of a great number of people" (verse 26). The smiths realize instantly what this will mean to their beach houses in Caesarea ... I mean, to the reputation of the great goddess Diana ... and so they become very upset and cry out, "Great is Diana of the Ephesians!" (verse 28).

This riot would have remained within the Goddess Makers Union Local #111 precinct had not the smiths rushed into the town square. Before long, they filled the whole city with confusion, and the people shouted for two whole hours, "Great is Diana of the Ephesians!"

Who cares about any of this? You do. Because Luke, the inspired writer of Acts, calls this mob a "church." Yes. He does it

Remains of the Ephesus theater.

three times—in Acts 19:32, 19:39, and 19:41.

The New Testament was written in Greek, and *ekklesia* is the Greek word Luke used here in Acts, chapter 19. (Our English equivalent is, "ecclesia.") It's the same word that the King James translators translated "church" every other time it showed up in the New Testament—112 times, to be exact. But they looked smack at the word in *this* context and choked on their English tea. How could they associate such a "holy" word as church with these heathen metalworkers? They couldn't. Yet there it was. What should they do?

They decided to do what they usually did, which was sacrifice consistency for the sake of their biases. Better to be inconsistent, they thought, than to associate church with these rioting maniacs. So they committed one of their many translating crimes and called this church an "assembly."

"I'm pretty sure we screwed up 'ekklesia' today."

I'm upset with these translators because, had they translated consistently and called this free-flowing mob a "church," they could have provided millions of people with a divinely inspired illustration of how loosely church *could* be conducted.

Take a glance at a *Young's Analytical Concordance* or a *Strong's Exhaustive Concordance* to see how many times these seventeenth-century Englishmen translated in accordance with their whim, rather than in accordance with God's vocabulary. They knew they should have been consistent with the Greek word *ekklesia*, but again, this word in this context shocked them.

These so-called translators associated *ekklesia* ("church") strictly with marble floors, hard pews, incense, and statues of the saints. That's why they couldn't bring themselves to also associate it with a riot. But it certainly can be associated with a riot, because the word *ekklesia* is a generic word. It's a ten-cent word the Greeks pulled from a paper bag at a downtown word store. Luke thought it a perfectly fine word to describe a riot. Well, the word simply means a group of people "called out." The prefix *ek* means "out" and *klesia* means "called." It is that simple, common, and unreligious. Here are two cheapo, paper-bag words welded together by the Greeks to describe people called out into the street, into the circus, into a beach party, into the community bath, into anything.

Nothing else is specified.

Why is this important? Because when people tell you to "go to church," what they mean is that you should go to a specified building at a specified time to do specified things with specified people. *Baloney.* Who gave them the right to make church that? God Himself puts no such limits on the word, and this inspired context from Acts proves it. God has a sense of humor, else He wouldn't have prompted Luke to use *ekklesia* to describe this riot. It's as if He knew it would drive the translators crazy.

Besides—and you should find this interesting—the Bible contains no such phrase as "going to church." Not once. Not one person in the Bible ever "went to church." How could they? The word *ekklesia* refers to people, not buildings. You can gather *with* people, but "going *to* people" is an awkward concept, indeed. You call out human beings, not piles of bricks. At least, no building I saw ever actually *attended* a riot. "Churches" breathe and shout and run around the marketplace in their togas; they don't sit on stone foundations and get steeples attached to them.

And yet someone may put forth this argument: "But you still need pastors and supervisors and teachers and such. Without these, you don't have church."

If this argument ever does cross your path, just do as I do. Say: "That's true, and not true. We do need helpful kinds of people in our lives, but who says we have to find these in the context of a brick building on Sunday morning? We can be supplied with these helpers no matter where we are."

It's true. When I've needed a "pastor"—that is, when I've needed someone to offer me practical guidance—God brings one my way. It may not be an "official" pastor ordained by humans (in my case I guarantee it won't be), but it will be someone God has given a natural heart for it. I will not meet the helpful-type person in a building on Sunday morning, but maybe in a Wal-Mart or a Starbucks on Monday afternoon.

I have friends who serve as pastors, supervisors, and teachers in my life. They don't have diplomas, and I sure don't call them "pastor" or "supervisor" or "teacher" (generally, I call them "Charlie," or "Matt," or "Sean," or "Clyde," or "Nelson"), but when I need them, I call them and they come. They're good at what they do. They're my friends. We talk, and I am helped. They've gone to the School of Real Life.

They're like Peter and John in the fourth chapter of Acts. When the big-shot, temple-educated leaders in Jerusalem called these humble followers of Christ before them to explain their behavior in the wake of Jesus' resurrection, the leaders were staggered. Acts 4:13—

> When they saw the complete assurance of Peter and John, who were in their view uneducated and untrained men, they were staggered, recognizing them as men who had been with Jesus.

My friends know the risen Christ. I dare anyone to produce a better qualification for service. My friends would stagger the minds of many institutionally trained clergymen. Why? Because the concept that God could produce wisdom apart from assembly lines is foreign to the clergymen.

So, what does a brick building on a Sunday morning have to do with any of this? Answer: Nothing.

Where did people pick up the one-day-a-week habit, anyway? Where did it come from? Why do so many millions of people think they ought to go to church once a week to worship God?

The once-a-week people camp around the fourth commandment God gave Israel on Mount Sinai, though I can't imagine why, because God says nothing in commandment four about going to church.

Commandment four says:

> Remember the Sabbath day, to keep it holy. Six days shalt thou labor, and do all thy work: But the seventh day is the Sabbath of the Lord thy God: in it thou shalt not do any work, thou, nor thy son, nor thy daughter, thy manservant, nor thy maidservant, nor thy cattle, nor thy stranger that is within thy gates. For in six days the Lord made heaven and earth, the sea, and all that in them is, and rested the seventh day: wherefore the Lord blessed the Sabbath day, and hallowed it

—Exodus 20:8-11, KJV

What is missing from this commandment is the very thing millions of people struggle to accomplish:

> Remember the Sabbath day, to make sure thou goest to church on it. Six days shalt thou labor and do all thy

work. Lucky thou, for the seventh day shall transform thee from laborer to slave—thou will be fighting seven natural instincts begging thee to stay in bed or drink orange juice on the sofa all morning with thy children.

Wake thy whole family before they want to get up. Wake thy son, thy daughter, thy servants, and any stranger unfortunate enough to be within thy gates. Thy cattle will think this is a day off; a swift kick to their hindquarters shall restore them to moral purity. The Lord thy God made the heavens and the earth and the sea in six days, then He rested on the seventh. *Thou* should be so lucky. The only time thou will be resting today is at red lights. Otherwise, it will be go, go, go, for thou. But thou should'st not worry. Thou can take a break on Monday when thou goest back to work.

I remember a church sign I saw a few years back in the little rural town I used to live in. This sign explained a lot about what Christians think worship is. Veterans Day was approaching, and the sign said:

"BECAUSE THEY SERVED, WE ARE FREE TO WORSHIP."

Not true, and let me explain. I am free to worship always and everywhere. I appreciate what our veterans have done and still do to keep enemies from our shores, but fighting for my freedom to worship is another matter. How could I ask these brave men and women to risk their lives defending a thing that could never be taken from me?

I can worship God in jail. I can worship God in a Chinese prison camp. I can worship God in a nation overtaken by militants of every persuasion. I can do this because true worship happens inside me. God's temple is in my heart, and I carry my heart with me wherever I go. Worship occurs in my spirit and nothing can stop that.

"Don't you realize that you yourselves are the temple of God, and that God's Spirit lives in you?" (1 Corinthians 3:16.)

This sign proves to me that Christians have reduced worship to gathering in buildings. Should a godless enemy overtake our country, the enemy will blow up all our churches and there will be no more buildings to gather in. The Christians will panic, because their worship centers around buildings. No buildings, no worship. That's what they think—and that's what the sign suggests.

There are many good reasons to fight for this country. The reason on the church sign is a bad one. No one should kill or be killed trying to preserve the one thing I can't lose.

All of a sudden, I'm thinking of church steeples: They're all wrong. The design is upside-down and dead opposite of what it should be. Church steeples have the wide part down toward the people and the point toward God, as if the church people have all these wonderful things to offer God, so much so that they need a freaking funnel.

It's God Who needs the funnel, not us. He's the One Who has so much to give. But church people are so busy pouring all their offerings out to God that they don't have the stillness of heart or the calmness of brain to see what marvelous things *God* is pouring out to *them.*

Churches have everything upside-down, and this sadness is reflected in their steeples.

Let's consult the apostle Paul on matters of church.

Paul is the man who took the good news of the grace of God to non-Israelites. Paul took the gospel of grace to people who were worshipping trees, planets, and possibly even multi-breasted goddesses. Did Paul tell them about the Sabbath day, to keep it holy?

No. The Sabbath wasn't *for* these people. The Sabbath day was part of the law of Moses, and the law of Moses came to Israelites only. Paul said in one place that the other nations didn't have this law (Romans 2:14). So did he teach it to them? No. He told them that they were justified in the sight of God, apart from works of law (Romans 3:28). So these people didn't even have to rest on the Sabbath, let alone go to church on it. The Sabbath had nothing to do with them, nothing whatsoever. (See my book about the apostle Paul and his gospel of grace, *The First Idiot in Heaven.*)

The Israelites in Jerusalem hated what was going on among the heathen with Paul. When they heard that thousands of idol worshippers were coming into the freedom of Christ without the law of Moses, their beards curled. Israelites from Jerusalem were always sneaking around Paul's people (after Paul left town), trying to trick them into religious bondage. It was the misery-loves-company principle.

Circumcision is a good example of what was going on back then. Circumcision was an Israelite rite requiring that all Israelite males have their leftover penis skin excised with a hopefully sharp knife. This rite was supposed to keep Israelites reminded that they were weak in the flesh without God. When you got circumcised, you were supposed to be embarrassed for the rest of your life. You were supposed to go around whining like a mouse: "Holy Moses, I've been circumcised."

But the Israelites got everything backwards, so much so that they actually became proud about being circumcised, and used it for bragging rights: "Ha! A section of my *penis* has been cut off! What about *you?*" The Israelites thought that because God had started the circumcision rite among them, now everyone should line up for it, otherwise they weren't any good. Certainly no one could be close to God without a surgically altered penis.

Paul once had a big meeting in Jerusalem with Peter (aptly named) and the other Israelite leaders about this. He took one of the ex-breast-worshippers (Titus, aptly named) to Jerusalem to show them what a fine believer this man was—and just look at his, um, *thing!* Listen to Paul describe the dramatic meeting (it really was dramatic back then) in chapter two of his letter to the believers in Galatia:

> Fourteen years later, I went up to Jerusalem again, this time with Barnabas, and we took Titus with us. My visit on this occasion was by divine command, and I gave a full exposition of the gospel which I preach among the Gentiles. I did this in private conference with the Church leaders, to make sure that what I had done and proposed doing was sound.

But no one insisted that my companion Titus, though he was a Greek, should be circumcised. In fact, the suggestion would never have arisen but for the presence of some pseudo-Christians, who wormed their way into our meeting to spy on the liberty we enjoy in Christ Jesus, and then attempted to tie us up with rules and regulations.

"We did not give in to those men for a moment, for the truth of the gospel for you and all Gentiles was at stake."
—Galatians 2:1-5

Good job, Paul. Way to keep those believers free from all sorts of religious entanglements. Way to promote the worship of Jesus in spirit and in truth.

Paul fought constantly with these Israelite false brethren. They never stopped hating the freedom that other nations reveled in—and it wasn't just freedom from getting your favorite reproductive organ shortened. It was freedom from observing the Sabbath, freedom from paying tithes, freedom from the rite of baptism—*freedom from every religious have-to you can imagine.*

I might add that this freedom was also available to the Israelites. But for some reason, most of them couldn't bear to drop their six-hundred pound barbells and catch Paul's train. That's strange, I think. On Paul's train, all you have to do is sit down and enjoy whatever view shows up outside the window. What kind of person would choose a six-hundred pound barbell over that? (A religious person, obviously.)

As I've just suggested, on another occasion the false brethren from Jerusalem got especially upset that the former statue worshippers weren't observing certain days—especially the Sabbath—and so they tried to trick the Gentiles into observing it. This particularly galled Paul, especially when some of his Gentile converts started buying into it. He wrote to the Galatians:

> At one time when you had no knowledge of God, you were under the authority of gods who had no real existence. But now that you have come to know God, or rather are known by Him, how can you revert to the weakness and poverty of such principles and consent to be under their power all over again? Your religion is beginning to be a matter of observing special days and months and seasons and years. You make me wonder if all my efforts over you have been wasted!
>
> —Galatians 4:8-11

Is there anyone out there being criticized for not doing some religious and holy thing for God? Are you hearing it because you don't go to church on the "Christian Sabbath"? (There's no such thing. The phrase "Christian Sabbath" doesn't exist in Scripture.)

Do your pseudo-Christian friends think you're headed for their version of hell because you haven't joined their club? Then quote them this corresponding passage from the apostle Paul:

> You, who were spiritually dead because of your sins and your uncircumcision, God has now made to share in the very life of Christ. He has forgiven you all your sins: He has utterly wiped out the written evidence of broken commandments which always hung over our heads, and has completely annulled it by nailing it to the cross. And then, having drawn the sting of all the powers and authorities ranged against us, he exposed them, shattered, empty and defeated, in his own triumphant victory!
>
> In view of these tremendous facts, don't let anyone worry you by criticizing what you eat or drink, or what holy days you ought to observe, or bothering you over new moons or Sabbaths. All these things are no more than

> foreshadowings: the reality belongs to Christ."
>
> —Colossians 2:12-17

This is a tremendous passage of Scripture. Don't let anyone worry you or criticize you for not observing certain days—including Sabbaths—or performing certain rituals. These things were shadows meant only to point to Christ, to suggest Him before He came. They were hazy pictures that would prepare people for the clear reality. Christ is the clear reality. When the reality comes, it's immature to live in the shadows. Really, it's stupid. It's like talking to the shadow instead of the person casting the shadow.

Christ has arrived. He is alive and sparkling with stars and comets. So why perform old, shadowy rituals like circumcision? Or baptism? Why be enslaved to Sabbaths and other holy days, when the Spinner of Planets occupies our midst and has unveiled new levels of grace? That's exactly what Paul is saying here: "Stop letting religious people bug you with all their rituals. They are living in the shadow, not the reality. The reality is Christ."

But didn't Paul start churches in all the heathen towns he went to? Certainly. But remember the definition of church; it's only a called-out body of people. As if to hammer home for us how spontaneous "ekklesia" is, Paul says nothing about his ecclesias meeting once a week, or gathering in a formal building with pews and a basement.

Paul loved the ecclesia in Corinth, Greece, for here was a well-established operation. However, notice what Paul wrote to these people:

"*If* therefore the whole church be come together into one place ..." (1 Corinthians 14:23, KJV).

From this, we know that it was *not* regular for all the believers in Corinth to come together in the same place at the same time.

This left room for God to freelance in their midst ...

At home, for instance. Paul wrote this to his friends at Rome: "Give my good wishes to Prisca and Aquila ...Give my love to the church that meets in their house" (Romans 16:3,5).

The church that meets in their house. If you need a verse to justify assembling at home, this one works well.

Here's another. This passage is surprising because it involves Peter and some other Israelites. Peter was in jail at the time, and "was closely guarded in the prison, while the Church prayed to God earnestly on his behalf." Why is this surprising? See where this church gathered. Following Peter's miraculous escape at the hands of an angel, Peter "went to the house of Mary, the mother

"Only three more rituals and I'm in."

of John surnamed Mark, where many were gathered together in prayer" (Acts 12:5-12).

Because going to church is supposed to be such a wonderful, holy thing, you would think that many wonderful, holy things would have happened in church, or at the temple of God. Not so. Here are some notable, New Testament events, and where they occurred:

> ▶ Jesus stills a storm—*on a boat* (Matthew 8:23–27).
> ▶ Jesus heals the sick and multiplies the loaves and the fishes—*on a hillside* (Matthew 15:29–39).
> ▶ Jesus declares Himself to be the Messiah—*at a well* (John 4:5–26).
> ▶ Jesus raises Jairus' daughter from the dead—*at home* (Mark 5:38–43).
> ▶ Peter raises a woman named Dorcas from the dead—*at home* (Acts 9:36–41).
> ▶ A Roman jailor and His family receive Christ through the teaching of Paul—*at home* (Acts 16:27–34).
> ▶ Mary, the sister of Martha, sits at the feet of Jesus—*at home* (Luke 10:38–39).
> ▶ A woman named Lydia and her friends receive Paul's teachings—*beside a river* (Acts 16:13–14).
> ▶ Jesus gives His soul for the sins of the world—*outside the gates of Jerusalem* (Hebrews 13:12).

To be fair, a few noteworthy events did occur at formal religious gatherings. One Sabbath day at the synagogue in Nazareth, the people tried to throw Jesus over a cliff (Luke 4:28-29). A little while later, at the temple in Jerusalem, several clergy members spit into His face (Matthew 26:67).

5.

Jesus would not "go to church" or join a religion

JESUS WOULD NOT "GO TO CHURCH" OR JOIN A RELIGION

Whenever someone tells me that they "got religion," I send them a sympathy card and a coupon for Pepto-Bismol. Religion is the enemy of good digestion. This is not to mention what it does to your social life. First, religion takes away your peace by making you worry all the time whether you've done enough for God. Then it takes away your fun, because you are certain God is watching your private thoughts on a giant screen. God can't believe how bad you are. You're an ill person—"A *sicko*," God remarks to a nearby angel. Then He shakes His white, hairy head, strokes His long, flowing beard, and wonders aloud to those at His right hand: "Where did I go wrong with (INSERT YOUR NAME HERE)?"

Religion is a bad thing, even in the Bible. In Acts chapter 17, the apostle Paul is in Athens when some toga-clad pooh-bahs invite him to address them on Mars' Hill. (This is the same place and the same time Paul said, "God does not live in man-made temples.") The first thing Paul says is:

> Gentlemen of Athens, my own eyes tell me that you are in all respects an extremely religious people. For as I walked through your city looking at your shrines, I even found one altar on which were inscribed the words, "TO GOD THE UNKNOWN." It is this God whom you are worshipping in ignorance that I am here to proclaim to you!
>   —Acts 17:22-23

The Greeks had several grand and terrifying deities who demanded constant invocation and sacrifice to keep them appeased. Paul knew there was but one God Who was now conciliated to humanity through the work of His Son, and so he was not complimenting these people by calling them "religious." See how Paul, addressing them, equated their religion with ignorance. Yet he was careful not to offend his hosts by using the two words in the same sentence.

The Greek word translated "religious" in this passage is *deisidaimon*. Paul spoke and wrote in Greek and this is the word he used. *Deisidaimon* is a two-part word: *deisi* = *dread* and *daimon* = *demon*.

Drop the weapon, I'm just the messenger. This is the Greek speaking, not me. I am innocent of the Greek language, and was not alive when any of this happened. It is nonetheless etymologically true: To be religious is to dread demons.

Isn't it a good thing, to dread demons? Not in the sense presented here. Demons are busy today turning people from God; it's their chief goal. The craftiest among them accomplish this, not through obvious evils, but through the agency of religion. They introduce subtle lies about God beneath the glow of stained glass; they reduce Christ's accomplishment to a challenge with the gentlest of twists. I will speak more on this in the next chapter. One who dreads demons in this context is one who *thinks* he or she is seeing the true God—and hearing true things about Him—but who in reality is seeing a misrepresentation of God, and hearing lies about Him as presented by demonic, whitewashed agencies.

"You think *you* have problems? I'm religious!."

The truth about the relationship today between God and humanity is found in 2 Corinthians 5:19—

> God was in Christ, conciliating the world to Himself, not reckoning their offenses to them (*Concordant Literal New Testament*).

Religion does its utmost to assure people this isn't so. Religion says: *You must still work hard to please God in order to atone for your offenses and rescue yourself from eternal torment or never-ending death.*

But no. This amazing rescue is a done deal. Because of Christ's work on the cross, God is now on friendly terms with the whole world. That's not me talking, it's 2 Corinthians 5:19. This is a glorious fact, and Satan can't do anything to change it. The one thing he can do, however, is lie about it.

Satan has succeeded magnificently. Well? Have you ever heard this truth announced in church? Have you ever been told that God is now at peace with the world? Rather, you've been assured that God is angry with the world—even believers are on shaky ground—and that He is prepared to damn any who fail to hurry up and believe in Him. This, in spite of Christ's sacrifice on the world's behalf. The caricature-God of demonic presentation will love you unconditionally—*as long as you love Him.*

Scripture does call Satan the father of lies (John 8:44).

If Satan can convince people that God still expects a concerted attempt at morality and devoutness by His followers—*or else*—he can get them so busy trying to *impress* this God that they never have the time or the energy or the peace of mind to stop and discover what God has already accomplished for them, through Christ.

Thus religion.

(In English, the word "religion" is derived from the Latin root, "lig," which means "to tie or bind." This, along with the Greek definition, should convince anyone that "religion" is a bad word. Knowing now that religion binds instead of frees, and inspires dread rather than happiness, there's no need any more to say, "I feel bound by my religion." It's a redundancy. Just say, "I am religious," and your Latin friends will know that you are in trouble. Those who know anything about knots will rush to untie you.)

Again, people in religions think they are toeing the line for God, when really they are toeing it for a demonic (and thus false) representation of God. God says: "I am at peace with the world." Satan, through religion, says: "God *can* be at peace with you—if you do the right things."

The religious person is constantly working; he or she has to be good enough to get into heaven and stay there. Never does the thought enter: *I am dreading demons.* But notice this about the people you know who are religious: They are fearful. They're afraid they are one misdeed away from disappointing their Deity. It's a slippery walk, and the supposedly angry God has a firm grasp on the edge of the rug. One false move and—*whaa-ooosh!*—out it comes. This kind of fear is not conducive to a peaceful life. It *is* an exercise in ignorance; God does not require anything of humans for salvation. (Even belief is a gift of God—Romans 12:2, Philippians 1:29—rather than a human achievement.) No one can gain it, no one can blow it. Salvation is "the free gift of God; and because it is not earned no human can boast about it" (Ephesians 2:8–9).

Who else but Satan could put a red bow on dread and make it look righteous?

This is a good time to note that I am not knocking anyone's religion; I'm knocking *all* religions.

Being religious, then, means unnecessarily dreading what God might do to you if you don't do something for Him. Make a sign of the cross or die. Kneel or die. Abstain from pork chops or die. Pray or die. Behave or die. Be baptized or die. Believe or die. Die or die. Love God or die. Every religion is different, but all religions accept those who meet their requirements, and damn those who don't.

Some religions demand human sacrifices. Others only want goats. Some, I suppose, urge the ingestion of poison. Some want monotonous prayers and chants. Some religions have forty-six requirements, some nine. The Christian religion generally demands only one thing: wisdom. You must be wise enough to choose Christ, or you die and stay dead until God resurrects you for an eternity of torment. The wise are saved; the stupid die and stay dead until their torture starts. This is also known as, "salvation by grace."

It makes no difference if your religion has a hundred requirements, a million requirements, or only one requirement. A requirement is a requirement, and requirements earmark religions. Religion is humans standing on their heads for God. The truth is that God is standing on His head for us. But people in religions are too busy doing *their* thing to even notice that God is doing *His*.

In light of all this, the pastor of a church once said to me: "Zender, you are making salvation cheap!" And I said, "I'm sure sorry. I didn't mean to do that, sir. I meant to say it was free."

As I already said, Satan's goal is to keep people from noticing what God has done for them through the sacrifice of Christ (that is, that He has saved them). Satan invented religions to accomplish this, and he hasn't recalled one of them yet for repairs. If these religions would advertise honestly, the standard pitch to the spiritual seeker would be: "You stand before us, a sinner, *un*saved. Now, here's what you must do to *get* saved. And you better hurry, because the distant Deity is tapping His watch and awaiting your next move. Ready? Set? *Do something righteous or die!*"

Christ's accomplishment is forgotten, and the dread begins.

The Christian religion, with its fun, its games, its social calendar, and lack of honest advertising, is the darling of Satan's heart. It is so near truth, yet still as far away from it as all the other religions: You still have to do something. That is, you have to drum up the proper kind of faith to be saved, or else.

But the Christian religion is worse than all the others because of how subtle the deception is.

Christianity boasts the name of Christ, the only name under heaven by which humanity is saved. This name gives the Christian religion a legitimacy other religions don't have. ("Hey, they talk about Christ, don't they?") Because other religions don't have the name of Christ, they must pad their deities with belly fat, bejewel them, or put them in charge of lightning, corn, or snow.

What other religion boasts the actual name of Christ? Never has self-salvation been so attractive, and so apparently acceptable. What other religion paints its tomb such a brilliant white? Thus, by means of this rollicking organization studded with Jesus jewelry and metal-fish appliqués, Satan has ensnared millions of nice, well-meaning people into believing in salvation by human effort.

Salvation by human effort is the essence of all religion, the source of all dread. Some may say, "But the Christian religion is exempt from this." It is not. In the Christian religion, believing is the effort required. You *must* believe, and you better hurry. This is what makes you stand on your head; you're desperate to believe, desperate to believe in the proper manner and with the proper frame of mind. This is what ties you up and makes you miserable. It's what takes your attention from God's accomplishment and focuses it on your own. You're full of dread, wondering, *Was I really in the right frame of mind that night at the altar call? Did I believe in the right way? Did I say the right words? Did I believe at all? Was my belief a sham? Am I really saved? Have I done enough for God? How can I be sure? Do I really love Him, or am I out only for myself?* These kinds of questions drive many serious Christians to worry, dread, and despair. This is precisely Satan's plan. Well, these *are* religious people, after all.

And so nice people (religious people) who would otherwise be turned off by the baser religions and the uglier means of salvation by human effort (cutting oneself, for instance, or ingesting poison, or abstaining from pork chops), line up to join Christianity.

It cannot be overstated: *Christianity is clean, neat, bright, and full of fun—and yet it is the same, in essence, as every other religion.* It's the whitewash that tricks you; all you have to do is "believe in Jesus," and then remember for the rest of your life the precise moment you managed that remarkable feat. But believing in Jesus is a work of the flesh (that is, it's a requirement for salvation), if it's the thing that *makes* you saved. The supposed innocence of "just believe in Jesus" is the whitewash that makes Christianity so seductive. The bones, however, are still inside the tomb because you still end up "saving yourself" by believing, not in Jesus, but in your ability to believe in Jesus.

Belief is important, but it's not what Christianity makes it to be. Personal belief doesn't save anyone. Jesus saved the world at the cross. Apart from divine intervention, believing in Jesus is impossible. None of us seek God on our own. In fact, we go out of our way to avoid Him (Romans 3:11–12). Personal belief is a gift of God (Romans 12:3; Philippians 1:29) that acquaints people with a salvation already won for them 2,000 years ago by Jesus Christ. And so, personal belief follows salvation, it does not precede it. If it preceded it, it would become a personal work that "gets you saved." But people aren't saved because they believe; they believe because they are saved.

This is why Christians come across so self-righteous and proud; *they* did something that the rest of the world couldn't quite manage. They try not to act self-righteous, but they can't help themselves. They're bursting with self-satisfaction and it oozes out their pores. Well, if you did something to save yourself from an eternal doom, what else *could* your pores do? This is exactly how Satan wants people to think, act, and ooze.

Here's Martin Zender's definition of Christianity:

Christianity is a religion of the survival of the wisest. It's a religion of people who are smart enough to save themselves by letting Jesus "save" them.

(If you post this on Facebook or e-mail this definition to your friends, don't forget the quotation marks around the second "save." You must retain the quotation marks there, because Jesus doesn't really save one who saves oneself by believing.)

And so, Christianity is the perfect religion for the humanist who wants to gild his or her humanism. With Christianity, the humanist remains the captain of his/her own destiny (he/she chose Christ), but also gets to damn those honest humanists who don't have gilding. Plus, the Christian gets to wear a robe if he/she is in the choir.

All of this is evil, but it is disguised as light. When I say "light," I mean that religion is sold as a good thing. It's dressed up in scents, robes, tambourines, and "feeling good about yourself." But Adolph Hitler also felt good about himself, so this gauge is unreliable.

Christianity is the most deceptive religion of all (I repeat that) because of how *much* false light is added to the same dark core of every religion: Do something to impress your Deity, or die. Few people in civilized nations who drive nice cars would go for such a ridiculous concept (the concept that creatures wearing underpants could possibly impress their Deity) unless it was dressed in righteous clothing. Give the damn thing an Easter bonnet, and people stand in line for it.

You want evil? Evil is the clergy asking mortal and sinning human beings to deliver themselves from their own mortality and sin by offering to God a living (immortal) and pure (sinless) faith—*out of their own mortal and sinning beings.* This is the ultimate evil, and quite possibly the ultimate stupidity. "Salvation from a human is futile" (Psalm 60:22, *Concordant Version of the Old Testament*).

Thus, religion is the best cloak evil ever had. And Christianity is the best cloak ever worn by religion.

How did this Christian religion get started? First, let's research the name "Christian."

Scripture says that believers in Jesus were first "styled 'Christians' in Antioch" (Acts 11:26, CLNT). There's something rotten about this word "styled" that accommodates the Greeks of Antioch, who were a sarcastic lot. "Styled" carries the connotation: "We don't know what else to call these idiots, so let's *style* them something."

The word "style" appears in Scripture only one other time, in Romans 7:3. The *Concordant Literal New Testament* tells of a woman who "will be styled an adulteress if she should be becoming another man's." The word carries that negative of a slant.

The word "Christian" appears only two other times in the original Greek Scriptures. In Acts, chapter 26, Paul defends himself as a prisoner of Rome in front of King Agrippa. Paul does a good job, too. He does so well that Agrippa says, "Much more of this, Paul, and you will be making me a Christian!" (verse 28). Paul just shrugs and says, "I would to God that both you and all who can hear me this day might become as I am ..." Then he adds with his usual sense of humor, "but without these chains" (verse 29).

Notice that it's the Roman king—not Paul—who uses the title, "Christian." Paul doesn't repeat the word. Instead, he says that he wishes Agrippa would, "become as I am." In all his letters, Paul never once referred to either himself or his friends as Christians. Paul hated formal handles like that. He and his friends were simply believers.

In 1 Peter 4:15–16, Peter writes that if anyone "suffers as a Christian he has nothing to be ashamed of and may glorify God by confessing Christ's name." Peter may have picked up the title for lack of a better one. It was not originally meant as a compliment.

I don't like the pigeonhole "Christian," and never use it. Look what it has come to describe. Answer "yes" to "Are you a Christian?" and you stereotype yourself as a person who hassles homosexuals, disdains Democrats, is chained to a church, and damns rappers and reprobates to hell.

I am not a Christian.

A Christian didn't used to be someone who practiced the Christian religion. (You've seen what a bad word "religion" is.) Being a believer in Jesus used to be free, not binding. You went to somebody's house, sat around, talked, prayed, and ate dates. No one made you sign a statement of faith. No one asked what church you went to. They only asked if you liked dates. If you didn't like dates, they had figs.

Here's what Christians mainly care about today: *What church do you go to?* Am I right? It's the first thing they want to know. You could have just come from a meeting with Jesus Christ. So what? The first thing someone will ask you is, "What church do you go to?"

"I just talked with Jesus."

"Yes, but what *church* do you go to?"

"You don't understand. I just walked on Lake Michigan with

the Son of God."

"I go to the Methodist Church on Elm Street. What church do *you* go to?"

It's all people care about. They want to label you. If they can't label you, they start scratching the backs of their necks. They're agitated. It bothers them that truth could live outside their box. It bothers them that people with Lake Michigan on their pants or clouds in their hair could have a real relationship with God.

"Jesus Christ just transported me to the third heaven, where I saw God!"

"Really? What church does *He* go to?"

Blame Constantine for all this. Constantine was the first emperor of Rome to become a so-called Christian. It's true that Constantine is the man who outlawed the persecution of those who believed in Jesus, but he also made Christianity an official, accepted religion. If the phrase "official, accepted religion" makes you want to grab a beer and watch football, you are rightly suspicious. As far as persecution goes, I'm all for feeding lions zebra meat instead of Uncle Harvey. But did Constantine have to build such a fancy cathedral?

Constantine is "credited" with building the first great Christian cathedral. Bad enough that truth had just dug a basement. Why did Constantine have to call it the Lateran Basilica? (I don't know what it means, but I bet it smelled like my grandmother's basement.)

I don't trust the whole thing. Constantine became a Christian in too strange a way for my comfort.

In A.D. 312, Constantine was gearing up for something

called the Battle of the Milvian Bridge. On the eve of battle, the emperor saw a vision. According to the historian Eusebius, Constantine saw a fiery cross floating in the middle of the sky. If that wasn't strange enough, underneath the cross appeared a phrase in Greek that read: "By this sign thou shalt conquer."

Constantine took this as a sign that, not only was Jesus Christ's cross on fire, but Jesus Christ Himself was guaranteeing that many of Constantine's enemies would graduate to corpsehood the following day.

Sweet success. The next day, Constantine killed a good many people of various non-Christian persuasions. "That settles it," Constantine said. "I'm a Christian."

In light of this, Martin Zender advises: "Whenever you see a cross in the sky, and the cross is on fire, and a string of words appears under the cross—*run.*"

I'm not saying that Constantine wasn't a good Christian. He was a very good Christian. According to several sources, Constantine had "many admirable qualities." Some troublemakers reading this may be tempted to ask, "What about in A.D. 326, when Constantine had his second wife, Fausta, and his oldest son, Crispus, put to death?"

I don't know. Maybe they were Democrats.

Today, the Christian religion has become to true believers what the God-vacated temple was to the first-century followers of Christ. Whatever it was to follow Jesus Christ then has degenerated into the popularity club of today. It's a new set of Pharisees and lawyers. They're still snakes and hypocrites, but instead of calling them that (as Jesus did) we have "Clergy Appreciation Month."

If you're a Christian today, you're in. Does anyone besides me see anything wrong with that?

Christianity today is more popular than Beatlemania of the '60s. John Lennon once noted that the Beatles were more popular than Jesus. That was the good old days. Now it's Jesus Who has all the screaming teenagers eating from His hand.

John, Paul, George, and Ringo used to strum their guitars (with the exception of Ringo, who played the drums) and shake

their moppy hair. The people went crazy by the thousands. The same thing happens in Christianity today except that the people on stage shake their Bibles, they have nicer haircuts, and the people go crazy by the millions. Other than this, how can I possibly compare Christianity with the Beatles? Today there are more T-shirts promoting Christianity than ever promoted the Beatles, making Beatlemania nothing at all like what is happening in Christianity today.

Jesus wrecked the tables of self-seeking people. He broke the wares of the people who used the temple for their self-gratification programs:

> Then they came into Jerusalem and Jesus went into the Temple and began to drive out those who were buying and selling there. He over-turned the tables of the money-changers and the benches of the dove-sellers, and He would not allow anyone to make a short cut through the Temple when carrying such things as water-pots.
>
> —Mark 11:15-16

The people no longer sell doves or change money in the church, but they still barter in esteem, power, and talent.

The organized church is first of all a social event. It is a place to be noticed for your clothes. It is a place to show off your family. It is a place to declare to the community: "I care." Or: "I am a decent person." Or: "I have skills this organization can use."

Figuratively speaking, people still cut through the temple carrying water pots. Whatever sustenance they need to feel good about themselves, church is their way to get there. The Jesus they worship is the Captain of their Self-Esteem.

But the pop-icon Jesus is not the Jesus of Scripture.

I have a friend named Marla who is well-loved and beautiful. She was popular in school, she's popular in the world, she's diva at the Spring Street Pentecostal Church in Columbus, Ohio. If there was a magazine called *Poise and Self-Possession*, this would be your cover girl. I know Marla must crack sometimes and weep into her woolen sweater sleeves, but she never shows a hint of that to anyone.

Marla is the gleaming Christian. She loves Jesus Christ, as long as she doesn't have to look stupid doing it. Sing in the

temple? Yes. Braid a whip and scatter the temple sales staff? Marla
has a hair appointment that day.

Rejection is definitely not what Marla wants out of life. She
knows deep down in some unreligious corner of her being that the
priesthood rejected Jesus Christ. *Church people rejected Jesus Christ.*
She knows it was the chiefs of the temple—not the bartenders at
the *Camel Ass Saloon*—who told the Son of the living God: "You
have a demon" (John 8:48, CLNT).

Pull out your compact, Marla, and drive away the impossible
thought. Jesus was from a different world, a different time. Marla
has worked hard to win acceptance in the community and in the
church, and she is not about to jeopardize that by heeding her still
small voice.

Here's the Jesus that Marla keeps away:

> He has no stately form or majesty that we should look
> upon Him, nor appearance that we should be attracted
> to Him. He was despised and forsaken of men, a man
> of sorrows, and acquainted with grief; and like one from
> whom men hide their face, He was despised and we did
> not esteem Him.
> —Isaiah 53:2–3, *New American Standard Bible*

This is the unwanted Jesus. The Jesus without a place today in
the religious fast lane. If this Man ever did show up in a modern
Christian church, all eyes would turn from Him. He would be the
strange one, the weird person, the troublemaker who would tilt
the system until all the alarm bells rang.

Unless Jesus wore a robe, a beard, a name tag, and turned
water into a non-alcoholic beverage, He would receive the right
foot of fellowship in nearly every Christian church in America. If
Jesus returned today without shepherd staff or halo, Christians

would hate Him. They will boil with anger at my even suggesting this. They will deny by shouting that they'd never do anything so terrible. But it wouldn't change a thing because they would do it anyway.

Enter Jesus, with His big ugly nose and thin lips, His spindly hands, and gangly stance. He comes to teach on His accomplishments at the cross. If the people could recover from His embarrassing appearance, they would certainly not tolerate His teaching. That would be the beginning of His slow death— His heralding of the cross and what it meant for *all* sinners. Jesus would say:

> God has allowed us to know the secret of his plan and it is this: He purposed long ago in his sovereign will that all human history should be consummated in Christ, that everything that exists in Heaven or earth should find its perfection and fulfillment in Him.
>
> —Ephesians 1:9-10

That would seal His fate, because Christians will not share their heaven with sinners. That's that, and their minds are made up. For Jesus, it would be just like in the old days, except the persecution would be cleaner. Larry would call Him into the pastor's office and say, *We really don't want you coming here anymore.*

Off He would shuffle to some farmhouse on Edwards Road, where other happy rejects would be waiting to hang upon His every word.

The agony Jesus experienced was being cast out of temples, not farmhouses. He never was kicked from a farmhouse in His life. It was the agony of being hated by the perfumed and the pious that made Him cry and sent Him to the mountains to pray.

Christians can't share this depth of suffering. They wonder

how they could. The world hates Christians for their hypocrisy, but that's nothing. Anyone can manage that. What is that compared with being hated by people who wear gold crosses around their necks? How does it compare with being hated by those who think they're doing Jesus a favor by persecuting you?

The suffering of Christ is the most terrible suffering there is. It's the pain of being persecuted by religious people. This kind of suffering can't happen to Christians. It can't happen to them, because Christians *are* the religious people.

What has happened to allow the despised face of Jesus Christ to be screened onto T-shirts and printed onto wall posters? Answer: Truth has left the Christian religion. The truth that Jesus loved is gone. Replacing it is popularity, entertainment, belonging, friendship, self-help, self-confidence, political involvement, professional music, rallies, screaming, crying, the wearing of gold crosses, the wearing of Jesus jewelry and T-shirts, and the marching of soldiers striving to save the world for God.

The really sad part is that all this is done in the name of the One Who would drive the lot of it from town with a homemade whip.

6.
THE CHRISTIAN RELIGION IS CONFUSING AND FULL OF HYPOCRITES

THE CHRISTIAN RELIGION IS CONFUSING AND FULL OF HYPOCRITES

Reporter: Sally, I'm one of those people looking for God. Right now, I'm considering the Christian religion. But is it true that, even though Jesus Christ came to take away the sin of the world—I'm thinking of John 1:29 here—sin will still keep millions separated from God for eternity? This troubles me.

Sally: Yes, that's true, Jim. People have to ask Jesus for forgiveness. Otherwise, their sins will haunt them forever.

Reporter: So Jesus really *didn't* take away the sin of the world?

Sally: He did and He didn't.

Reporter: Can you explain that?

Sally: Sure. He takes sin away for people who ask Him. He doesn't for people who don't.

Reporter: But this verse says He does it for the *world*. It says, "Behold the Lamb of God, Who takes away the sin of the *world*."

Sally: I know that's what it says, but it doesn't mean that.

Reporter: How come?

Sally: This is a Christian mystery.

Reporter: What constitutes a Christian mystery?

Sally: Anything we don't understand and shouldn't think about.

Reporter: I've heard that Jesus came to undo the devil's work. All evil. This interests me.

Sally: Yes! I love that truth. You're thinking of 1 John 3:8.

Reporter: Yes. But isn't it also true—according to your belief—that the devil will lead most of humanity to hell, where they will be damned forever?

Sally: Yes.

Reporter: But if the devil does this, how is it that Jesus has undone his work?

Sally: (plugging her ears) A-maaaa-zing graaaaaccccce...

Reporter: Sally! This is serious. I need to ask you something concerning my niece.

Sally: I've never been to Nice.

Reporter: No—my *niece.*

Sally: Oh. All right.

Reporter: My niece Judy was a very loving person. My brother and his wife read Bible stories to her as a child. They took her to church. One evening three months ago, they asked her if she had made a personal decision to accept Jesus. She said—and my brother will never forget this—"No, not yet." Sally, *that very night*, my niece was killed in an automobile accident.

Sally: How awful. I'm sorry. How old was she?

Reporter: Fifteen.

Sally: I'm sorry to hear that.

Reporter: Why?

Sally: If she had been eleven or twelve, she might have had a chance. But she was old enough to know better.

Reporter: To know *what* better?

Sally: Maybe we better not talk about this.

Reporter: You must tell me.

Sally: Your niece had a chance to accept Jesus, but she didn't take advantage of it.

Reporter: (stunned) *Salvation is of chance?*

Sally: Yes. I had a chance and took it. I won. Judy had a chance, too, but she lost.

Reporter: But I thought Jesus came to save sinners. And according to what others have told me, not accepting Jesus is certainly a sin.

Sally: It certainly is a sin. It's the worst kind of sin, and your niece was a sinner, for sure. But you misunderstand; Jesus only saves those who accept Him.

Reporter: But doesn't one have to quit sinning to accept Him? I mean, if unbelief is a sin, wouldn't belief be the cessation of sin?

Sally: (reaching for her ears again) A-maaaaa-zing graaaaaaaacccccce ...

Reporter: Sally! Basically, you're telling me that Jesus only saves "sinners" who quit sinning.

Sally: (relaxing her fingers for a moment) ...who quit sinning long enough to accept Him.

Reporter: But they have to quit sinning for at least that brief moment.

Sally: Okay, for at least that brief moment! But He still saves sinners, and nothing you say will make me change my mind.

Reporter: Where is Judy right now?

Sally: You've put me in an awkward position. I don't really like sharing this part of The Good News, but I'm an evangelist-in-training, so okay. From the moment your niece died, she has been tortured in hellfire. She has already suffered these few weeks more than I will suffer in a lifetime; I don't know about *you* yet. And her agonies have only begun.

Reporter: But I thought God loved Judy!

Sally: He does, but love is tough. Wouldn't *you* have a loved one tortured for eternity if they didn't appreciate *you?*

Reporter: No! Not for five minutes!

Sally: Well, you're not God. God's love is not our love. This is why Christians are to fear God and keep His commandments.

Reporter: Because of what He will do to them if they don't?

Sally: Fear and threats are all part of The Good News.

Reporter: And these make you praise the Lord?

Sally: A hundred times a day! *You* should praise the Lord.

Reporter: How *can* I praise the Lord, if what you told me is true?

Sally: You have to train your mind to stop thinking about Judy.

Reporter: I can't!

Sally: That's because you're not a Christian yet. If you go to heaven, you'll be able to stop thinking about *everybody* in hell. Won't that be great? I'm practicing for it now. You really should accept Jesus. He's a wonderful Savior!

Reporter: Wonderful?! It doesn't sound like He does too damn good a job.

Sally: You said a curse word!

Reporter: #@✂☹! ☠☀✝☎! ↝☀! How do you like *those* curse words? I haven't said those in years!

Sally: (plugging her ears) It's awful! Stop! Amazing grace!

Reporter: Your doctrine is driving me to it! This so-called "good news" is not bringing me peace. It's making me upset and mad at God.

Sally: *What?*

Reporter: Take your fingers out of your ears! I said, your gospel is not making me feel very good. It's not drawing me to God.

Sally: That's because you're not a Christian yet. You need to accept Jesus, and you better hurry up before you die.

Reporter: Does Jesus accept *me?* Is Jesus my Savior?

Sally: That depends.

Reporter: Depends on what?

Sally: It depends on whether or not you *believe* He's your Savior.

Reporter: He's not my Savior until I *believe* He's my Savior?

Sally: That's right.

Reporter: Why would I want to believe something that isn't true?

Sally: Huh?

Reporter: You just said that, until I believe, Jesus isn't my Savior. Don't start singing now, but why would I believe something that isn't true?

Sally: But it is true.

Reporter: *What's* true?

Sally: Jesus *is* your Savior.

Reporter: Boy, that was quick; He changed His mind already. Now let me decide if I want to believe that or not.

Sally: No. You don't get it. If you *don't* believe, He's *not* your Savior.

Reporter: Sally, please. I want to believe what's true. If it's true that Jesus is my Savior, I would want to believe that. If He's *not* my Savior, I'm certainly not going to be so stupid as to believe something that isn't true. So quit hedging on this. I need to know. Is Jesus my Savior or isn't He?

Sally: I *told* you! He's not your Savior until you *believe* He's your Savior.

Reporter: *Damn!* Now He's not my Savior again!

Sally: You said a curse word again!

Reporter: I couldn't help it.

Sally: Look. Everything depends on what you do.

Reporter: Ahh! Now we're getting to the heart of it. *I* control whether I'm saved or not.

Sally: I didn't exactly say that.

Reporter: But that's the logical conclusion.

Sally: Logic is of the devil! I rebuke you, Satan!

Reporter: But you just said that everything depends on what I do.

Sally: It does.

Reporter: But I thought salvation was a free gift.

Sally: It is! Salvation *is* a free gift. It's grace! And grace is a free gift. Free, free, free! You can do *nothing* to save yourself. Nothing, nothing, nothing!

Reporter: But you just told me my salvation depends on what I do!

Sally: It does.

Reporter: Sally, I think I just found myself a new religion.

Sally: Praise the Lord!

Reporter: No, praise Budweiser. My new religion is beer.

Jesus accomplished many fine things on the cross for the sake of the whole world: "Our advocate before the Father is Jesus

Christ and He is just, the One Who made personal atonement for our sins and for those of the rest of the world as well" (1 John 2:2).

Satan can't do anything to ruin this, but he can do a lot to keep people from knowing about it. Satan's main weapon is hypocrisy. He packs this hypocrisy into the pill of false teaching. Then he grinds that pill into a batter of confusion, cooks it on the griddle of religion, and serves it every Sunday with organ music and good singing. (It has to look good, taste good, and sound good, or people won't swallow it.)

If you think Satan is a mythological figure, try to start my car. I don't give Satan more power than he has, but I don't sell him short, either. He doesn't have a pitch fork or a pointy tail like the Christian tracts paint him. Satan loves that caricature. Why shouldn't he? He invented it, and he distributes it through the unwitting cooperation of the many Christian tract companies.

Satan loves for people to think of him in a red suit with a black goatee. This cartoon image keeps the world from realizing who he really is and what he really does. Think of who has foisted this Looney Toon image on the world and made the world laugh at God: the Christian church.

Satan is a spiritual being who poses as an angel of light. Satan's master agents do not disguise themselves as ministers of obvious evils. No, but they disguise themselves as ministers of righteousness (2 Corinthians 11:12-15). This means that Satan works chiefly in churches, not in bars. He deals in steeples and stained glass, not in alcohol or cigarettes. I'm not saying he doesn't sometimes use beer and tobacco, but these are not how he turns the world from God.

Satan's goal is to turn the world from God. He wants people to look at God and say: "What an idiot." Does alcohol turn the world from God? No. People addicted to alcohol generally turn *to* God. What about war? God is the soldier's only friend. Does pornography turn the world from God? No. A man does not look at the picture of a naked woman and say, "God is an idiot."

Satan turns the world from God through hypocrites who say, "My salvation is nothing of myself," and then who point to unchurched people and say, "It's their own fault they're going to hell." He turns the world from God through hypocrites who say, "Salvation by faith is of grace," and then who damn the world for faithlessness.

He turns the world from God through Christian television.

The Trinity Broadcasting Network is Satan's greatest success story. What's with the golden thrones, the props, the plants, the robes, the stage shows, the mascara, the crying, the hellfire, the canned reverie, and the breathless pride? Pride drips off people's hair gel on this network. The world sees right through this gunk. People whose brains still work watch television like this and think: "If these people represent God, God must be a total idiot."

How true.

Golden thrones, robes, breathless pride, and phony reverence: Welcome to Satan's playground. Satan is not Darth Vader. At his best, he will not outwardly scare you. If he scares you, he can't deceive you—and he wants to deceive you. Deception is his main thing, but he can only properly deceive you when you're off your guard and enjoying his presence.

Satan shaves regularly. He wears a suit and a tie, and drives a nice car. He's very enthusiastic about his job. He pats little children on the head and smiles into anything with a lens. (Hello, Joel Osteen.) There are purple curtains behind him, a beautiful choir in front of him, and gushing green plants all around him. But as soon as you lend him your trust, he upends everything true

by reducing God's accomplishment to an offer and His grace to a threat.

That Satan operates through what appears to be light and righteousness today is too fantastic for some to believe (that is, for those who have never seen Christian television). So I quote a passage of Scripture, from Paul in 2 Corinthians 11:12-15—

> I am determined to go on doing as I am doing, so as to cut the ground from under the feet of those who would dearly love to be thought of as God's messengers on the same terms as I am. *God's* messengers? They are counterfeits of the real thing, dishonest practitioners masquerading as the messengers of Christ. Nor do their tactics surprise me when I consider how Satan himself masquerades as an angel of light. It is only to be expected that his agents shall have the appearance of ministers of righteousness.

No one would mistake a Buddhist monk for a messenger of Christ. An orthodox Jew could not be mistaken for a messenger of Christ. No one sees a Zulu tribesman in deepest Africa and thinks, "He is a messenger of Christ." Who would mistake an atheist, a Satan worshipper, or the ACLU for one? Only persons called "Christian" could be mistaken as messengers of Christ.

Thus it is Christians—and no other people—who are the unwitting carriers of the most horrible "gospel" ever invented: Love God or be tortured for eternity.

> In "that day" many will say to Me, "Lord, Lord, didn't we preach in Your name, didn't we cast out devils in Your name, and do many great things in Your name?" Then I shall tell them plainly, "I have never known you. Go away from Me, you have worked on the side of evil!"
>
> —*Jesus Christ*, in Matthew 7:22–23

The name "Christianity" is *only* a name. Today, it is a harbor for demons who hate humanity. These demons terrorize humanity through the false teachings of God's "friends." Christianity is the front, the whitewashed wall, the polished cup. Christianity is the wolf in sheep's clothing. It is everything the Pharisees were in the days of Jesus.

> Apparently you cheerfully accept a man who comes to you preaching a different Jesus from the one we told you about, and you readily receive a spirit and a gospel quite different from the ones you originally accepted.
> —*the apostle Paul, in* 2 Corinthians 11:4

Naming the name of Jesus does not guarantee truth. Don't be fooled by people who say "Jesus" all the time. That name is often a Hollywood wall with nothing behind it but old two-by-fours.

There is the real Jesus, and there is "a different Jesus." I have heard people say, "We love you, Jesus!" But what most of them love is the *concept* of Jesus. They love the emotional, pop-icon Jesus and the buoyant feeling this Jesus gives them. They've tried everything else and could never find comfort. Then they tried Jesus, and He made them feel good. He filled their emotional vacuum. They love how it feels to be in love with this Jesus. In their pictures of Him, He is handsome and fit, with a well-trimmed beard, flowing hair, and a winning smile.

This love affair is even warmer if others don't have it. "My Jesus, My Jesus" is the lover's song. This assumed monopoly (on His favors) brings worshippers to ecstasy. They honor Him with their lips, but clamp their teeth hard on their traditions. These, they cannot let go of.

> You hypocrites, Isaiah described you beautifully when he wrote, "This people honoureth me with their lips, but their heart is far from me. But in vain do they worship me, teaching as doctrines the precepts of men."
> —*Jesus Christ, in* Mark 7:6–7

Today we call it lip service.

Tradition is the lover here, not truth. These kinds of people have received a different spirit and a different gospel from the spirit and gospel of the true Jesus. Belonging to an affirming social community is the seat of their affection. Social acceptance and a spiritual veneer is the trophy for every sacrifice made for their Jesus.

The trouble is that Jesus is not in the traditions. He is not in the churches. His spirit and gospel are far better than what passes here for godliness. Jesus has long since left these structures of stone. Christian traditions damn the very people Jesus came to save. So—why would He be in church?

The churches are worshipping a different Jesus. The true Jesus is gone from the Christian religion.

And so I exhort you: Go to the hillsides and to the lakeshores. Go. Go far from the temples and find Him now.

I do not hate religious people, so no one should think that. It's the religions that I hate, not the people in them. I hate the systems that bind the people. I hate the false and contradictory teachings and what these teachings do to the name and character of God. I hate that these religions turn thinking people who would otherwise embrace God, *from* God. I'm angry at the demons that torment my friends with guilt if they miss church. I hate that this dread is covered by whitewash and made to look God-like. I hate Christian radio and television because of the false information given to seeking people. I can't stand to think that people are actually listening to the Christian broadcasts and thinking that what the people on the broadcasts are saying about God is true.

This is the main reason I have to write.

I know that there are many wonderful and sincere people who are stuck in the mud of religious bondage. Many wonderful and sincere people feel they have to go to church every Sunday. Many wonderful and sincere people think that God saved them because they worked up enough faith to impress Him. Many wonderful and sincere people think that their evil Uncle Harry is burning in hell right now. Many wonderful and sincere people think they have to lower themselves into a lake, or make a sign of the cross, or abstain from Hershey bars in March in order to be right with God. None of this changes the fact that these same people are wonderfully and sincerely dead wrong.

Peter is a good example of this, and one passage from the book of Matthew will prove what I'm telling you:

> Jesus began to explain to his disciples that He would have to go to Jerusalem, and endure much suffering from the elders, chief priests and scribes, and finally be killed; and be raised to life again on the third day.

Then Peter took Him on one side and started to remonstrate with Him over this. "God bless you, Master! Nothing like this must happen to you!" Then Jesus turned round and said to Peter, "Out of my way, Satan! ... you stand right in my path, Peter, when you think the thoughts of man and not those of God."

—Matthew 16:21-13

How sincere can a person get? Peter was only trying to help. He sincerely wanted his Master to live. Peter exhibited the enviable human traits of concern and compassion. He even gift-wrapped these in the modern Christian cliché: "God bless you!"

Jesus was terribly impressed: "Out of my way, Satan!"

And so Satan is where we would not ordinarily expect to find him.

Unfortunately for Peter, he was dead out-of-sync with God's plans, and so Peter had *unintentionally* become an adversary of God. (The Hebrew word *satan* means, "adversary.") Jesus ignored the sincerity and tunneled to Peter's core: *You're not with the program, son.*

This passage proves that a person can be the most sincere, most well-meaning, most cliché-ridden Christian at the Elm Street Holiness Gospel Tabernacle, and still be clueless as to God's agenda.

Or worse.

"Now the spirit is saying explicitly, that in subsequent eras some will be withdrawing from the faith, giving heed to deceiving spirits and the teachings of demons, in the hypocrisy of false expressions" (1 Timothy 4:1-2, CLNT).

The Trinity Broadcasting Network, Joel Osteen, Rick Warren—along with the rest of Christianity—stand guard in their golden parapets, spying the countryside for deceiving spirits and teachings of demons. These are our self-appointed protectors. Armed with gilded Bibles and laminated bookmarks, they are poised and ready to kill apostasy when it comes (apostasy means, "to fall away from true faith"). But they won't kill it, not unless they're suicidal. Because the apostasy is in their own camp; they will never see it because they *are* it.

This is strange and disturbing, but it is not a new thing. Some of the Israelites of Jesus' day had the same sickness. They scanned the world for religious evil. Did they find it? Oh, yes. They found people who forgot to wash cups before drinking, who forgot to say prayers before eating, who wore wrong-colored tassels in the temple. After putting everything in order, they killed their Messiah.

Jesus put it this way:

> Alas for you, you hypocritical scribes and Pharisees! You are like white-washed tombs, which look fine on the outside but inside are full of dead men's bones and all kinds of rottenness. For you appear like good men on the outside—but inside you are a mass of pretense and wickedness.
>
> Alas for you, scribes and Pharisees, you utter frauds! ...You are blind leaders, for you filter out a mosquito yet swallow a camel.
>
> —Matthew 23:23–24, 27–28

Let's follow these creatures and see where they lead.

The world spots hypocrisy in the Christian religion. See?

"Accept God's grace. damn you!"

It's the big furry beast with the fourteen humps: "*My* salvation is unearned, but *you're* damned because of something you didn't *do*." This is complete contradiction. It's naked hypocrisy with fourteen humps. Keep reading it until you see it. One reading should do. Yet those in the Christian religion can read it a dozen times and still not detect the hypocrisy. Why? Because they're too sidetracked swatting the hundreds of little mosquitoes that trouble them daily.

Christians have a mission to get *Playboy* out of department stores and prayer back into schools. They're swatting some mean bugs, it's true. But what about this mutant camel wrecking Tokyo?

The world is so sick of Christian hypocrisy. They're sick of hearing about "grace" in one breath, and "damnation" in the next. They're sick of the strange Christian god who loves people unconditionally, up until the time he damns them for not loving him back. This is why normal people roll their eyes every time "Christian" is mentioned. They're thinking to themselves: *Here comes the camel again.*

The Christians, however, can't see the multi-humped monstrosity. They are blinded to the creature that clings to their backs and paws their scalps. When the Christians sit down to consider the problem—to wonder why people reject their literature, turn off their television shows, and rebel against their morality campaigns—they think: *We must need more preaching*. But this is much like Captain Smith of Titanic fame thinking: *We must need more icebergs*.

How does Satan manage such a wonder? How does he manage to get so many people blinded to what hypocrites they are?

He uses diversions. Satan does to Christians what Hogan used to do to the Germans.

It's the *Hogan's Heroes* syndrome. I hope you remember the popular, '60s sitcom about Allied soldiers in a German prisoner of war camp. If so, then you will recall how Colonel Hogan and his men used to set fires on one side of Stalag 13, then break prisoners out of tree stumps on the other side. These were the famous diversions. Klink and Schultz were so busy putting out the little barrack fires that they didn't notice the giant escape hole outside the west gate.

Satan does the same thing with Christians. He gets many of them so busy fighting lesser fires over *here*, that he is able to work a worse evil in their midst over *there*.

Satan loves that Christians can't see their own folly. Why shouldn't he? Satan masterminded the whole thing. Remember 1 Timothy 4:1-2:

> Now the spirit is saying explicitly, that in subsequent eras some will be withdrawing from the faith, giving heed to deceiving spirits and the teachings of demons, *in the hypocrisy of false expressions.*

How can you tell a demonic teaching from a non-demonic one? There's a simple test that anyone can apply: Look for hypocrisy. This is as objective as it can be. Wherever you find people saying one thing (false expressions) while meaning another thing (hypocrisy)—and disguising the whole mess as righteousness—there are demons and deceiving spirits at work.

It's that simple. It's that dependable of a test. It works every time.

I'll say it again: The hypocrisy of false expressions is what earmarks demonic teachings and deceiving spirits. This is the smoking gun. The best thing about this is that you don't have to take my word for it, or anybody else's. See for yourself. Just look for the gun with the smoke coming out. The smoke is hypocrisy.

Look for the hypocrisy. Any normal person can see it.

We are living in the era of which Paul prophesied. "Withdrawing from the faith" cannot refer to the world, because the world can't withdraw from something it never had. These spirits *must* afflict the visible church—and they do. (It will help to remember that the two elements of the Greek word translated religious are—in English—"dread" and "demon.")

This is the era of spiritual deception. Maybe you didn't realize how vast it would be, or how righteous it would appear, or how many people would fall for it. You may never have dreamed that this deception would carry the very name of Christ. I know how incredible all this must seem to you. But which is more incredible: that millions of people claiming to be followers of Jesus are actually unconscious dupes of Satan embarked on an emotional and self-serving tangent that appears to everyone except them to be hypocritical self-righteousness, or that nearly an entire priesthood of holy people who alone knew the Scriptures and exercised themselves daily to recognize the Messiah, killed Him when He came?

I offer the table on the following page, the smoking gun. This table lists just some of the hypocrisies and false expressions that *characterize* the Christian religion. Tell me if I'm wrong.

This table should be funny because of how true it is. It should be thrilling because of how naked the errors stand before us. But it's not funny; it's not thrilling.

It takes a powerful spirit to make a person say one thing and mean another thing. It takes a deceiving spirit to make a person say one thing and mean the opposite thing. It takes otherworldly intelligence (the cream of the demonic spiritual crop) to make the person who says one thing while meaning the opposite thing to not even notice the hypocrisy.

THESE ARE THE SCRIPTURAL TRUTHS ADVERTISED BY CHRISTIANITY	BUT THESE ARE THE THINGS IT ACTUALLY TEACHES
There's nothing you must do to be saved.	Here is what you must do to be saved.
You are absolutely, totally helpless to save yourself.	You must make a wise decision in order to be saved.
God controls all things.	Every person on earth has power to thwart God's intentions.
We can't boast about going to heaven.	If you go to hell, it's your own fault.
Love never faileth.	The love of God cannot overcome human stubbornness.
Human beings are in bondage to sin.	Human beings are free to choose God.
Grace is unmerited favor.	Grace is given only to those who merit it with faith and obedience.
God is the savior of all mankind.	A good percentage of mankind will spend eternity in hell.
God's love is unconditional.	God loves you as long as you meet certain conditions.
God's will is unstoppable.	Anyone can thwart God's will.
Salvation is not a thing of chance.	There is no second chance to be saved.
God has good news for you.	Most of mankind will perish forever.
God loves you.	God loves you as long as you love Him.
Christ died for all sin.	Christ died for all sin except the sin of not believing He died for all sin.
The Good Shepherd seeks the last sheep until He finds it.	The Good Shepherd seeks until it's too late.
God's justice was satisfied in the cross of Christ.	God's justice demands eternal torment or annihilation.
Jesus Christ is greater than Adam.	Jesus Christ will not save everyone Adam condemned.

What it takes to fashion all this into an attractive religion that snares millions of well-meaning and otherwise intelligent people, and drives the rest of the world from God, is beyond my grasp, and I don't even want to behold that creature.

7.
THE CHRISTIAN RELIGION FITS ITS OWN DEFINITION OF A CULT

THE CHRISTIAN RELIGION FITS ITS OWN DEFINITION OF A CULT

People in church are very busy. They are busy fighting the world, fighting themselves, and fighting God. But no one in their right mind wants to fight the world, fight themselves, or fight God. These things go against every natural instinct. All normal people want to do is sit down and be quiet. They just want to sit down and be alone for an hour or two, and thumb through a magazine. After this, they want to hang out with friends. Maybe they will order a drink, eat some restaurant-style chips, and laugh together. After this, they just want to go home and go to bed.

What does it take to get people fired up to do things that every natural instinct tells them not to do? It takes three things: (1) a battle cry, (2) a board of directors, and (3) central heating. Or air conditioning. If you're going to issue a battle cry and get people to come hear you cry about it, you better keep them cool in the summer and warm in the winter.

I have not mentioned file cabinets and telephones, but I intend to do that now. This is where the board of directors comes in, because the board can order these things and make sure that they bulge and ring, respectively. Recent studies performed with rats at an Office Max in Minneapolis have proven that people will simply not gather to your battle unless they can determine that you have at least six file cabinets, three telephones, two LCD projectors, a laser printer, and a secretary named Phyllis. And you better keep Phyllis cool in the summer and warm in the winter.

I'm just telling you these things in case anyone asks.

People love strong, centralized organization, especially if it has different-sized rubber bands. Strong, centralized organization makes people feel good. If you've got three pizza-eating teenagers running truth out of a downtown warehouse (across from the Elks Club and in-between Domino's Pizza and Tattoos By Rick), don't look for crowds. But put lies in an office suite with Phyllis and several Mediterranean ferns (a blue-tinted water cooler helps), and people will beat a path to your doorman.

I told you in the previous chapter that Satan runs religions. We have already seen that religion means "dread-demon," and that the chief purpose of all religion is to make people dread what God might do to them if they don't do a certain thing. We learned that the Christian religion is no exception to this, in that you must recollect the precise moment you accepted Jesus (this is the "certain thing" you must do), or you will be sent to hell for eternity, where all the rubber bands are the same size.

I said at the end of the previous chapter how smart Satan must be to make otherwise intelligent people say one thing, mean the opposite thing, and not realize they're doing it. But he must really be smart to make people fight the world, fight themselves, fight God, then tell the rest of us how much peace they're having.

Not really. All he needs is (1) a battle cry, (2) a board of directors, and (3) central heating.

From this dynamic trio, he can easily fashion a cult.

What is a cult? The first dictionary definition of a cult is, "a particular system of religious worship, especially with reference to its rites and ceremonies" (The Random House Dictionary of the English Language, College Edition).

You were expecting Charles Manson and Spahn Ranch?

The key words here are "system," "rites," and "ceremonies." People love this stuff. Systems, rites, and ceremonies make people feel all warmish inside. They give them that special sense of belonging to something larger than themselves. People slip into systems, rites, and ceremonies like they slip into hot tubs.

The apostle Paul warned his friends that Satan's lies are deceptively packaged: "We are not meant to remain as children at the mercy of every chance wind of teaching, and of the jockeying of men who are expert in the crafty presentation of lies" (Ephesians 3:14).

Instead of "the crafty presentation of lies," the *Concordant Literal New Testament* has, "the systematizing of the deception." Like this:

> We should all attain to the unity of the faith and of the realization of the Son of God, to a mature human, to the measure of the stature of the complement of Christ, that we may by no means still be minors, surging hither

and thither and being carried about by every wind of
teaching, by human caprice, by craftiness *with a view to
the systematizing of the deception.*

—Ephesians 4:13-14

That's more literal, and it paints a more diabolical picture.
Satan knows that law-abiding citizens with recessed sprinkler
systems in suburban America and Canada will not fall for lies that
limp grease-soaked out the back end of a downtown garage. He
is far too intelligent for that. Satan is a master packager. People
love protocol, and Satan knows that. People love the comfort
of systems, good lighting, and smooth pews. Therefore, Satan
has systematized deception. This makes the deception easier to
swallow.

A system is the candy shell that coats the bitter pill.

Human beings are Satan's agents in accomplishing all this.

All this seems to clash with what I've been saying. I've been
telling you how much pressure going to church puts on people.
It's still true. The churches know about this pressure. That's why
they do things to compensate for it. They have to make the
pressure seem worth it. I'm not even saying that they're doing
this on purpose. They do it instinctively. They, themselves, need
pampered and protocoled, so they give the same thing to their
people.

This is where central heating comes in. This is where mauve
carpeting comes in. This is where good music and an aura of
holiness (air fresheners, actually) help soothe the harried soul.

Do you have a high-pressure job? Then I bet you also have
paid vacations and medical benefits. The more your job will kill
you mentally, the more benefits come with it. Why do you think
businesses are willing to pay you for weeks of not working? That's

stupid. Why do you think they offer to underwrite your kid's tonsillectomy? That's ridiculous. It's because no one in their right mind would work for your company without serious incentives.

This is where the religious system kicks in and does its thing. Now is when the rites, the ceremonies, the comforts, the hugs, and the handshakes arrest the intelligence long enough to get devotion from it. There's another helpful vignette of religion: *Religion is the art of arresting the intelligence long enough to get devotion from it.* Devotion to what? To the peaceless cause.

"Don't think, just come. We will take care of you." Before you know it, you're stuffed with deviled eggs and acoustic guitar solos. All to keep you from thinking. Because as soon as you start to think, as soon as you face your fears, as soon as you ask your forbidden questions, you rock the boat. *And look: You just made the potato salad slide off the table.*

The disturbing thing about all this (the belonging, the system, the rites, the ceremonies, the food, the fun, the fellowship, the just-believe-what-we-tell-you mentality) is that it sounds an awful lot like a cult. If we're to take this dictionary definition of cult seriously, there appears to be only a fine line between a cult and a modern Christian church.

Or is there?

No one wants to be in a cult. Those who are in cults don't even know they're in them. But they're sure that everyone else is in a cult. Everyone is pointing. Everyone is in a cult except the people who are pointing. But, again, everyone is pointing.

I am here to stop all this pointing. There is now an easy and sure-fire method of telling whether or not you or your loved ones are in a cult. Simply buy a book called, *Larson's New Book of Cults,* written by Bob Larson, published by Tyndale House Publishers of Wheaton, Illinois.

Larson is a noted Christian radio and television personality, and Tyndale House publishes Christian books. Christianity, with Larson as its representative, has made itself an authority on identifying cults. This is a lucky day for the rest of us, because Larson and company have saved us a lot of work. We're just as lucky as first-century Israelites whose leaders told them: "You people just relax. *We'll* tell you when the Messiah arrives."

Bob Larson's picture appears on the back cover of his book. Right next to Larson's picture, someone wrote:

Encyclopedic in form, popular in style, *Larson's New Book of Cults* analyzes dozens of cults and movements from historical, sociological, and biblical perspectives. It will tell you what you want to know about the cults' origins, their appeal, and their strategies. Most important, it details how each cult deviates from Christian truth.

Did you see what already happened in Larson's book before we could even appreciate Larson's picture? "*It* will tell you what you want to know." That's nice of *it*. "Christian truth" is already set up as the standard by which all cults are measured. Even before page 1, Larson has tossed objectivity out the stained-glass window by assuming that the people in *his* group can't be a cult.

I wish he had said that Scriptural truth was the standard by which all cults are measured, but he didn't. And he couldn't, because by the standard of Scriptural truth—well, I will just stop there for now. We must proceed slowly.

Religious people will hear that you are reading this book and they will say to you: "Stop reading that book. Martin Zender is a cult leader." Really? What cult leader ever says, "Don't believe anything I tell you"? But that's exactly what I'm telling you right now. I am inviting you to analyze the objective details—put forth by the Christian religion itself—of what defines a cult. If I am a cult leader, then I will fit the profile. However, If Larson's *religion* fits the profile—well, I'm getting ahead of myself again.

According to Bob Larson, one of the characteristics of a cult is: "discouraging natural curiosity." Naturally, you were curious about a book titled, *How to Quit Church Without Quitting God*. But your religious friends don't want you reading it. Why? What are they afraid of? Are they afraid of truth? I think they are. I think they're literally afraid of truth. They're afraid of the potato salad sliding off the table. Why are they already exhibiting one of the characteristics of a cult? That's a good question. I'm not even going to answer it; it's your brain here, not mine.

Do you remember that Old Testament passage when Elijah challenged the prophets of the false god Baal to a "God contest"

(1 Kings, chapter 18)? Each contestant built an altar, sacrificed an animal, and challenged their Deity to consume the sacrifice with fire. Whichever deity answered the call was the true Deity. In case you don't know, Elijah won the contest, and the prophets of Baal retired in shame. (Well, actually, Elijah slaughtered them wholesale, but let's just stick with the retirement scenario.)

In the spirit of Elijah, I am hereby challenging the Christian religion to a cult contest. I am going to take all nineteen of Bob Larson's characteristics of a cult and apply them, objectively, both to his religion, and to myself. I'm going to do this in front of everyone. I'm not going to be like Bob Larson, who turns the light away from his own camp. I've got nothing to hide. So welcome aboard. The rules of this contest are simple: Whoever scores the most points, wins (i.e. "loses"). Fair enough?

You are about to see things with your own eyes, and smell them with your own nose. Larson's list of cult traits is thorough. It is detailed, specific, un-dodgeable. How objective can one get? This list comes from Bob Larson, who represents the Christian religion itself. This list does not originate with Martin Zender, his children, his sister, or any of his associates. Martin Zender is only going to quote Bob Larson, shine the light all around, and then leave.

Think of me as a reporter on the scene. I am only going to describe for you what I see, and how things are. I don't have to be an expert at anything to do this. There will be no need for you to rely on my intelligence during any part of this report; I'm glad to be relieved of the pressure.

Bob Larson has unfortunately made his religion the standard of truth, the Mother of All Cult Detectors. By doing this, he has deflected suspicion from his religion. This is not a new trick. By setting themselves up as The Official Messiah Detection League, the Pharisees of Jesus' day deflected all suspicion that they, themselves, could have missed the Messiah.

I have already shown you how Christianity became an official religion 1,700 years ago. I showed you what the word "religious" means. I demonstrated for you on a chart how the Christian religion claims to believe certain truths, while actually teaching the opposite things. You saw this with your own eyes. You've experienced it in your own conversations with Christians. You have already seen for yourself how confused these people become whenever they try to answer your simple questions about life, death, hell, the work of Christ, and the fate of unbelievers. All I have done is confirmed for you things that you've already suspected, but that you couldn't quite put your finger on. Something has been rotten in Pew-land, you just haven't known what.

I need to say this again: The hallmark of the Christian religion is contradiction. It hugs you, but it can't look you in the eye. It promises you illumination, but it can't give you straight answers to your deepest questions. It advertises a loving and all-powerful God, but ultimately can't deliver Him. It guarantees you peace, but gives you worry. It claims to have the light, then shrugs and says, "God is a mystery."

I wonder if any of these things characterize a cult?

"Even given the current anti-cult climate, few targets of the cults see their future as one of involuntary slavery and physical domination. Before joining any exotic sect, one should be aware of what could result: neurosis, psychosis, suicidal tendencies, guilt, identity confusion, paranoia, hallucinations, loss of free will, intellectual sterility, and diminished capacity of judgment. It will be much easier to avoid such consequences by identifying and recognizing the following psychological forms of 'cult-coercion'" (*Larson's New Book of Cults*, pg. 16).

(All of the following numbered paragraphs are quoted directly from Bob Larson's book. All items in these paragraphs are word-for-word reproductions of Bob Larson's points.)

1. Absolute loyalty. *Allegiance to the sect is demanded and enforced by actual or veiled threats to one's body or eternal spiritual condition.*

Does the Christian religion fit this bill? Christianity is the only sect I know of which, if you don't join it—or if you join then think about quitting—threatens you with eternal torture. *Eternal torture*, for God's sake. How is *that* for a bodily threat? Is that bodily enough for you? In some churches this threat is

veiled. In other, more honest churches, they dare to tell you to your face: "If you do not accept Jesus (that is, accept Him according to *our* terms, according to *our* statement of faith), *then you are lost forever.*"

Talk about coercion! How much coercion do you want? Jesus. How many people go to church today just because they're afraid that if they don't go, their "spirituality stock" will plummet and God will send them to their pastor's version of hell? Larson also writes on page 16: "Young adult cult recruits are the least likely to consider thoughts of abandoning the group ... Any consideration of leaving immediately conjures guilt feelings of forsaking God's calling, falling into Satan's hands, or even worse, risking the wrath and judgment of God."

Why wouldn't these kids feel this way? *It's exactly what pastors and priests tell them will happen if they quit the Christian religion.*

Does Martin Zender fit this bill? God likes you, whether you buy my book or not. You can even buy it, then throw it away. As for me, you can love me or leave me. You can even love me, *then* leave me. None of this human activity will affect God's opinion of you. That's because God sees you—even you—through the sacrifice of His Son.

It's the divine activity that counts here.

"God was in Christ personally reconciling the world to Himself—not counting their sins against them" (2 Corinthians 5:19). Are you part of the world? Then you are included in this. God is *not* counting your sins against you, not even the sin of unbelief.

God sent His Son to die for the sins of the whole world, not just for the sins of Christians. This upsets the Christians. To me, the amazing thing is that Christ's work *includes* Christians. For here are some of the most self-righteous people on earth.

God did His best for humanity at its worst. The proof of God's amazing love is: while we were *sinners* Christ died for us (Romans 5:8). Therefore, you, a mere human being, cannot undo God's plan for you or the work He accomplished on your behalf through Jesus Christ before you were even born. This work stands, not because of you, but in spite of you. In spite of you and me. God's love does not consider the worthiness of its object. That's God's love. God loves because He *is* love, not because any of us are lovable. God loves because He likes to do it. His love is based on favor, not merit. If it was based on merit, my dog would get it, and I'd be screwed.

What if you don't believe in Jesus Christ right now?

Relax. It is not yet your time to believe, but your time will come. Even if you don't believe in Jesus now, God will one day give you belief. I know this, because "God is the Savior of all humanity" (1 Timothy 4:10). We just don't see the fruit of His work all at once. "For there is one God, and one Mediator of God and humans, a Man, Christ Jesus, Who is giving Himself a correspondent Ransom for all, *the testimony in its own eras*" (1 Timothy 2:6, CLNT).

You cannot believe in Jesus unless God moves you to believe. I have no idea when it will happen for you. It may not happen in this lifetime. *It may not happen in this lifetime.* But it will happen. This lifetime is not all there is in matters of salvation. Who ever said it was? The pope? Pastor Bob? Some Mascara Queen on TBN? They do not know the true Jesus. They do not know the Scriptures. They are of a different spirit and they teach a different gospel. The fullness of God's grace is not even revealed until ages to come. That's not me, it's Ephesians 2:7. God must become "All in all" (1 Corinthians 15:28).

Score
Christianity: 1 Zender: 0

2. Altered diet. *Depriving one of essential nutrients and enforcing a low-protein diet can lead to disorientation and emotional susceptibility.*

Does the Christian religion fit this bill? Although it doesn't force people to eat junk food, the modern Christian religion is famous for sugary treats and emotional people. What a coincidence. Anybody ever heard of a roast beef social? I didn't think so.

Someone sent me a brochure from Trinity Church in East Lansing, Michigan. Appreciate this entry under the category, *For Parents of Children*: "400 dozen cookies will be needed for the 400+ children expected to attend this year's Vacation Bible School!" The exclamation point at the end of the sentence is a harbinger of things to come. This baking frenzy will add up to a dozen cookies per child. What I would want to know is: *Who's bringing the insulin?*

Speaking of sugar, the most Christian of the so-called Christian holidays is Christmas. Sugar is the goddess of Christmas. Christmas is an eating orgy, and sugar is the mistress of ceremonies. The other great Christian holiday is Easter. Easter is a very meaningful time when people celebrate the resurrection of Jesus by eating vast amounts of chocolate in the shape of bunny rabbits.

Does Martin Zender fit this bill? Martin Zender does become discouraged occasionally and eats too many roasted peanuts. But as a rule, I do not fit this bill. In fact, my diet has continually improved my entire life. I have become a champion of eating well and of helping those friends of mine whom I wish to live a long time, to eat well also.

I spoke at a conference a while ago in Michigan. The two guys who went with me ate chocolate bars and drank pop the whole way up. I drank water and ate leftover beef from a baggie. I ribbed my friends about their diets, and the fact that they were putting on weight and would die soon. This only made them want to buy potato chips.

The people at the conference were mostly over fifty years old and ate like mature adults. (My companions could only stare at them in wonder.) This made them clear-thinking and emotionally stable (the people at the conference, not my companions). It's a challenge addressing clear-thinking, emotionally stable people. They don't laugh at all your jokes. They don't cry at all your sentimental stories. But when they do laugh and cry, you know it's you and not Starbursts.

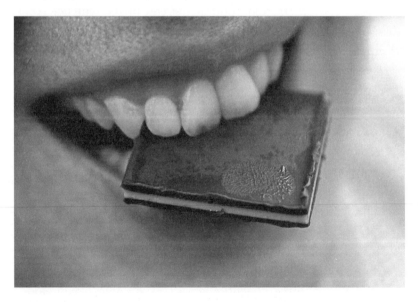

Score
Christianity: 2 Zender: 0

3. Chanting and meditation. *Objective intellectual input is avoided by countering anti-cult questions with repetitious songs and chants.*

Does the Christian religion fit this bill? I call it the "Shut-Up-And-Sing Syndrome."

Congregant: Excuse me, Pastor Bob. Is it true that my dead daughter is burning in hell right now?

Pastor: Shhh! Can't you see it's time for *Gabriel Jones and the Sucrose Singers?*

Singing is taking over the Christian religion. If you want to pack a church, just advertise that some singers are coming. Better yet, sing a song about the singers coming. Because here they come: gospel singers, inspirational singers, *Reverend Don and the Singing Pastors, Boys From Bethany, The Mother of God Hip Hop Family Singers.* It doesn't really matter what kind of group it is or what instruments they play, as long as they play and sing.

We did a lot of chanting in the Catholic church. It was ridiculous. We said the same words over and over again every week like robots:

Priest: Lord have mercy.

Us: Lord have mercy.

Priest: Christ have mercy.

Us: Christ have mercy.

Priest: Lord have mercy.

Us: Lord have mercy.

Nobody dared ask what this was all about. The priest noticed me squirming one day and asked me later in the vestibule:

Priest: Are you asking for trouble, Martin?

Me: Lord have mercy?

Priest: I better see you behaving yourself next week.

Me: Christ have mercy!

We couldn't get away from this chanting business. I call it the "Shut-Up-And-Chant Syndrome."

Does Martin Zender fit this bill? Don't get me wrong. I'm not against singing. I know that David played the harp and tambourine and sang all kinds of great songs and hymns. I like good singing. Harps are nice, too. I just think singing has become the focal point in Christian churches. There's too much singing. Enough singing, already. Can't people just roll up the fifty-foot lyric screen (with all the repetitious lyrics) and talk about God for awhile?

I used to emcee a conference once a year in Ohio. I focused on helping people understand God. The ratio of singing to teaching was one part singing, nine parts teaching. If people wanted more singing, they could go out to their cars and listen to the radio.

I don't like Christian music. I'll admit that I do like the beat of some of it, but most of the lyrics—when one can make them out—are sappy. I am a classic rock guy, so I could potentially like Christian music that sounded like The Beatles or Blondie, but I don't get much out of the lyrics. I can't make them out. What are these people saying? The words are all garbled. Why can't these people just play their cool-sounding songs, and then tell us about God when the songs are over? I can't concentrate on lyrics (supposedly the heart of Christian music), when a synthesizer is knocking my ears out and the drums are banging like World War III. (With Led Zeppelin, it doesn't *matter* if the drums are banging like World War III, because who cares what the lyrics of *Whole Lotta Love* are? All we want is to hear Jimmy Page's epic guitar solo.) How can I understand the testimony of these musicians when I'm jamming to a heavy bass line? I can't mix the two. Give me God, or give me ZZ Top. But for God's sake, don't try giving me both.

Score
Christianity: 3   Zender: 0

4. Conformity. *Dress, language, names, and interests take on a sameness that erodes individuality.*

Does the Christian religion fit this bill? Praise the Lord, it does. Praise God. Hallelujah. Thanks be to God. (I'm just reporting here.) Thank you, Jesus. Praise the Lord and bless this Easter bunny to the use of our bodies. Amen and hallelujah.

Some Christian churches like to call everybody "Brother" and "Sister." It's not "Mr. and Mrs. Smith," it's, "Sister Louise" and "Brother Ed." But when they really get to know you, it's just "Brother" and "Sister." If they don't call you "Brother" or "Sister," you're still not one of them. For instance, if a visitor comes to church—Mahmoud Ahmadinejad, say—no one would call him "Brother Mahmoud." He would have to earn that title by either signing the statement of faith or booking *The Tehran Gospel Trio*.

Only certain sects of the Christian religion dress alike, unless we want to count the common choir and the robes of its members, and maybe we should. Amish people all wear the same dreary clothes. I saw some young Amish girls selling bread at a roadside stand one day, and they frightened me. They all wore black capes and black bonnets that stuck way out from their faces like horse blinders. It was unnerving; I half expected them to levitate. I felt bad for them.

Does Martin Zender fit this bill? Nobody ever calls me "Brother Martin." It sounds like the name of a monk, a thing I could never be:

"Brother Martin, will you fill these stone jars with rotten pickles?"

"Yes, Brother Dominick. As soon as I finish listening to *Whole Lotta Love*."

Score
Christianity: 4 Zender: 0

5. Doctrinal confusion. *Incomprehensible "truths" are more readily accepted when presented in a complex fashion that encourages rejection of logical thought.*

Does the Christian religion fit this bill? Confusion is the glue that holds Christianity together. How could Bob Larson write this and not laugh out loud at his own religion? Christian doctrines crash together like trains in the night. Engines explode, couplers snap, boxcars roll end-over-end down the hill. When the dust settles, the trainmasters look up with a smile and say, "This was *not* a train wreck." Then they pull out their LCD projectors and lecture you on the history of trains.

I have a book called *Trusting God* (published by NavPress, 1988). Author Jerry Bridges spends the first sixty-six pages asserting God's sovereignty over people. As this train builds speed, Bridges brings another train around the bend on the same track, head-on toward his first train. This occurs on page 67, when Bridges insists upon "people's freedom and moral responsibility."

As the wreckage smolders about him, Bridges brushes off his pants and then, on page 69, calmly quotes one Richard Fuller, the third president of the Southern Baptist Convention: "It is impossible for us to reject either of these great truths, and it is equally impossible for our minds to reconcile them."

In other words, no thinking allowed here. This is not a train wreck, it only looks like one. Everything makes perfect sense. Just close your eyes, click your heels together three times, and believe what we tell you: Both these opposites are true. God controls you, *and* you are free of His control, all at the same time.

I know that many of you will be tempted to bring your logical thinking to this Christian mystery. Don't do it. Logical thinking does not work here. Did you not hear the eminent Baptist? This task is impossible for your minds, so leave your brains at home. This wreck that is not a wreck is too marvelous for the mere reasoning powers of humans. We're not in Kansas anymore, Brothers and Sisters. Reject logical thinking. Reject logical thinking! (Wasn't this one of the traits of a cult? Oops.)

Another incomprehensible Christian truth is that God is God, but He's not responsible for evil. That is, He's running the *entire* universe—well, except for those forty-nine billion bad things that happen every day. The only way theologians can explain this (without reaching a conclusion, for theologians do so dearly hate conclusions), is to present the "truth" of the "puzzle of evil" and the "problem of evil" in as complex a fashion as possible. I'm not saying this is consciously designed to confuse the hell out of people, but that's the result.

In his book *The Many Faces of Evil* (Zondervan Publishing House, 1979, 1994), John S. Feinberg begins chapter 2, "Theonomy and the Problem of Evil," this way:

> In this chapter, I will explain how a problem of evil arises for a theonomous theology and show that a theonomous system can solve its problem of evil. Moreover, I plan to show that not every theonomous system must incorporate the same account of ethics. After briefly introducing theonomy, I will present in depth the views of one theonomist, William of Ockham, as a concrete example of a theonomous theology. I will then explain how a problem

of evil arises in relation to theonomy and how theonomy solves it. Finally, the chapter closes with some meta-ethical comments.

—Pgs. 23-24

Wow. Meta-ethical comments. If I had meta-ethical comments, I would surely put them at the beginning of my chapter, not at the end.

I have another book titled, *The Puzzle of Evil* (HarperCollins, 1992) by Dr. Peter Vardy, lecturer in the Philosophy of Religion at London University's Heythrop College. After 203 pages, Dr. Vardy concludes: "I accept that God is Almighty, but by this I do not mean that God is able to exercise total power in the world."

Of course not. We understand, Dr. Vardy. Otherwise, you would have to be consistent and make sense, which would offend every ethic of your dark profession.

Another book of mine, *Encountering Evil* (John Knox Press, 1981) contains "live options in theodicy." According to the advertising copy on the back cover, "Six outstanding Christian philosophers and theologians" offer "a compendium of insight and scholarship" on "the ultimate dilemma."

Hmm. Let us see.

On page 8, John K. Roth writes:

> Prior to death, and perhaps beyond, existence is in process. Because things move and change, waste may not be simply waste, nor evil simply evil. Capitalizing on that fact, some writers mute screams of pain by hearing them as *instrumental*. Destruction then becomes a means to what is new and better. Or, if not all havoc readily fits that scheme, ruins may still provide occasions for atonement, forgiveness, and magnificent attempts at redemption. To

the extent that evil can be interpreted as instrumental, as somehow transcended by a better situation overall, power's waste is rendered less radical.

On page 39, John H. Hick writes:

Since a theodicy both starts from and tests belief in the reality of God, it naturally takes different forms in relation to different concepts of God. In this paper I shall be discussing the project of a specifically Christian theodicy; I shall not be attempting the further and even more difficult work of comparative theodicy, leading in turn to the question of a global theodicy.

On page 104, David R. Griffin writes:

I now turn to the solution I favor, to which the rejection of *creatio ex nihilo* is fundamental. In fact, the problem of evil is uniquely a problem for those theistic positions that hold the doctrine of omnipotence implied by the doctrine of creation out of nothing. For, the problem of evil can be stated as a syllogism validly entailing the non-existence of deity only if deity is defined as omnipotent in the sense of having no essential limitations upon the exercise of its will. And it is precisely omnipotence in this sense that the speculative hypothesis of *creatio ex nihilo* is designed to support.

Does Martin Zender fit this bill? Huh? Martin Zender begs you to bring your brain to his book. I have not asked you to believe something simply because I say it is true, but because I have laid out the facts.

I *want* you to investigate and think critically. Because the closer you look and the more rationally you think, the more you will see that I am right. I am not right because I'm better than you. I'm not right because I've attained some mysterious gift that you'll never have. I'm right in the same sense a news reporter is right when he describes the same train wreck that you, yourself, are looking at. Or, on the positive side, when he describes a sunny day that's streaming into your own window.

There is no such thing as an incomprehensible truth. Truth is understandable and makes sense. Children understand truth.

Accepting truth is another matter.

God says many true things in His word. These things are not only true, but understandable. The problem is that many of these truths clash with what humans *want* to be true. So instead of simply believing God, some members of humanity (especially those with theology degrees) tend to hold onto what God says *and* to what they want to be true.

This is what ruins perfectly good trains.

Bridges is right when he says God is sovereign. If God isn't running the universe, we're all in trouble. God is the One "Who works out all His purposes according to the design of His Own will" (Ephesians 1:11). That's *His* own will—not yours, or mine, or Bridges,' or eight billion other people's.

God running the universe is very easy to understand. So is this: "[God] is the One who gives to all humans life and breath and everything else" (Acts 17:25).

Any questions? People with Winnie the Pooh lunch boxes understand all this perfectly.

Bridges destroys his case when he lets his feelings and traditions crash into truth. Bridges doesn't *feel* God's hand, so he assumes he's over here and God is over there. That is, Bridges assumes he's acting freely, apart from God's influence. Have you ever felt certain that your car was going to start? Then it didn't. What does this teach you? You can't trust your feelings.

Bridges doesn't like the thought that God gives him *everything*. It hurts his pride. Oh, well. Gravity hurts *my* pride, but so what? I still fall down.

People who can't believe God's simple statements point to places in Scripture where people are doing things, willing things, riding their donkeys to Bethlehem. Bridges would say, "Look! This person is believing God. That person is *not* believing God. This person is willing to come to God. That person is riding his donkey to Bethlehem."

I see all these things happening, Jerry. All these verses are true. People do things and will things every day. I decided to write this book. You decided to go to the grocery store. Your sister decided to accept Christ. So?

The mistake you make is assuming that all these people are acting freely, without a cause. Didn't anything cause me to write this book? Didn't anything cause you to go to the grocery store? Didn't anything cause your sister to accept Christ? Keep tracing this buck and you'll be standing in front of a Very Big Desk. (In other words, God is the cause of all causes. Humans yield to the strongest influence—every time. And God is ultimately behind every influence. Piglet can reason from there.)

Thousands of Scriptures show people doing things. But these Scriptures don't often tell *why* the people are doing the things. Do their actions have a cause? Yes. The two passages I quoted earlier that the Pooh people understand, lift the veil. There is an ultimate cause behind everything. There is an ultimate reason why all things happen. The cause and the reason is God.

Where is the rain coming from? You say it's coming from that big cloud; your mom says rain comes from God. Who is right?

Both of you. But you're stuck in the troposphere; your mom looks through that to the ultimate source.

▶ God is governing all of earth's affairs.
▶ You can be free of God's governing.

Both things cannot be true. The absolute truth is: God is governing all of earth's affairs; He's God. The relative truth is: You make decisions and do things.

All trains now arrive at their destinations. You have a will, it's just not free. God is the cause, you are the effect—but the cause is invisible. This is what throws people off. Don't let invisibility throw you off. Don't let God's invisible hand make you think He's out of town.

Now evil. The theologians sound drunk to me. They're all trying to impress one another with their knowledge. Knowledge of *what?* None of them make sense. They write like idiots. Theology is the only business in the world where formal schooling makes you stupider in it.

God created evil. Here is another simple statement: "I create evil." I didn't write that. It's Isaiah 45:7. My eight year-old nephew understands it.

But the theologians say, "God can't do that because God never sins." So who said God sins? Who said evil was sin? How many calories does a theologian burn when he jumps to a conclusion? Enough to consume an Easter bunny? A marshmallow egg?

Evil is not necessarily sin. Evil is the Hebrew word, *ra*. All this word means is, "to break" (Parkhurst Hebrew and English Lexicon, pg. 656). That's it. In the Bible, the Israelites called the desert "an evil place." How can a place sin? It can't. So it's the context thing again, just like with the word "church." This verse proves that evil has no moral bias. A place can't sin. You can't send a desert to confession. A desert can't pee its pants inside a small, shadowy closet. By saying that the desert was an evil place, the Israelites meant that the desert was broken-down and wasted.

To "sin" means to miss the mark. It's the Hebrew word *chata*. This is a different word from *ra*. God creates *ra*, but He never *chatas*. God never sins. And so God could create evil without sinning, as long as He meant to create it and it worked toward His greater purposes. God *did* mean to create evil and it *does* work toward His greater purposes. I'll tell you how in a moment.

See the theologians.
See the theologians attempting to reconcile their doctrines.

Because God created evil on purpose, He didn't sin when He did it. It's the theologians who make God a sinner. They say that evil threw God for a loop. God planned a perfect universe, but then evil broke down the back door and sent everyone running. God turned around so fast that the end of his beard cracked like a whip. God said, "What the—"

Everything's been messed up ever since.

So now God is scrambling to keep up with evil—or so they tell us. God hopes He can salvage something. He hopes some people cooperate with Him, but most of His plans are mincemeat now.

This Christian theological view makes God a sinner, not my view.

I'm quite upset because this is the picture painted for us by the Christian religion: Ever since evil barged unannounced into

God's universe, God has been trying to make the best of it. His big, fat fingers are crossed as He tries to save His jolly old universe from being a total embarrassment to Him. He sent a cure that only works if you want it to: Jesus.

The traditional, old-school Jesus of Christianity is a morose, wanna-be savior who poses for painters with a glowing heart on His chest

and two fingers held up, slightly bent, as if He's not strong enough to keep them erect. Jesus looks sad in all the portraits. Very mopey.

Why? Because His Father's plans are basically screwed now. Not very many people like His Father. Millions reject His Father's plan. It makes Jesus wonder why He went to the cross for God. I'd be sad, too. The cross was a lot of agony for such a lousy turnout. How could anyone even crack a smile under such circumstances?

Christians are the ones who make God a sinner, not me. He planned, He failed, He dialed 911. He's doing the best He can.

It's not very good.

In contrast to all this horror, here's the simple "secret" of evil: God needs to break things because He can't demonstrate His ability to fix things if nothing ever breaks. God can't raise people from the dead if nobody ever dies. God can't save people unless they're lost first. God can't comfort people who have never been miserable. God can't show love without a backdrop of hate. No one can feel good for eternity without feeling lousy for a few brief years.

Evil provides contrast. That's it. It's no puzzle, and no mystery.

("God has all humans penned together in the prison of disobedience, that He may have mercy upon them all"—Romans 11:32; There's some contrast for you.)

Go ahead and burn another Easter bunny. Jump to the conclusion that most of the people you know (some of whom you love) are going to end up in hell for eternity. If you do jump to that conclusion, you *can't* appreciate the purpose of evil. Evil will make you despair. It may even make you kill yourself. If you think that a majority of the universe ends in chaos (that is, that there's a place where your mother, father, or unbelieving children will be writhing in pain for eternity), then you *can't* trace evil to God. You can't believe God's simple admission: "I create evil." (Unless you're a Calvinist. Only Calvinists can swallow the hairball that God created evil on purpose so He could eternally torment people

He refused to save.)

You either have to make *people* responsible for evil, or the devil. The devil is an easy scapegoat. But if you make the devil sovereign in evil, then you have another God. No, sorry; it's worse. The devil God becomes greater than the God God because the God God can't stop the devil God. (If God can stop the devil, why didn't He do it before all this happened? Christians tell us salvation is secure. How? They also tell us that Satan derailed God's plans in the Garden of Eden. So how is salvation secure? Who's to say Satan won't derail God's plans again? And again? If it happened once, it can happen again. And again. And again. So God can't control things. *That's* comforting. I think I'll go to bed now and sleep like a baby.)

My answer to *this* horror is that God will eventually return everything to Himself. This happens through Jesus Christ's work on the cross and nothing else. Read Romans 11:36 and Colossians 1:20. Read these verses and go to bed. The judgment verses are still in the Bible, but judgments are a *process* toward God's goal. Judgment is *not* the goal. That would be stupid. The verses I just gave you are the goal. Judgments *lead* to goals, and the goals are always good. That's the way God works. God, Himself, is good.

God won't *just* return everything to Himself. Then what would be the use of going through all this misery down here in the first place? Everything returns to God richer and fuller and brighter than when it left. This happens because of the experience of evil.

Evil is temporary; happiness is forever. The temporary evil buys the eternal happiness. This eternal happiness is for everyone— eventually. Eighty years or so of freaking misery, mixed with some joy, some roast beef, and Led Zeppelin songs. Half of it you're sleeping. Then an eternity of happiness to follow. You can't be eternally happy unless you've been temporarily sad. It's all about contrast. This makes sense and it's the best deal going.

It's the answer to evil.

If you don't believe this truth, you either have to refuse to think about what you do believe—eternal misery for most of the world—so you can sleep at night, or you have to adopt some asinine theology with lots of syllables that answers nothing and confuses even yourself.

The permanence of evil is the biggest lie of the Christian religion. The best thing that can be said about most Christians is that they refuse to think about what they believe. It's a credit to them. Congratulations to them for not thinking. Now, if we can only get them to quit writing books.

Score
Christianity: 5 Zender: 0

6. Exclusivity. *Those outside the cults are viewed as spiritually inferior, creating an exclusive and self-righteous "we" versus "they" attitude.*

Does the Christian religion fit this bill? *We* are believers, *they* are unbelievers. *We* chose Christ, *they* did not. *We* are saved, *they* are damned. *We* will be floating in conditioned air for eternity; *they* will be writhing in flames. *We* will be singing (and singing and singing and singing); *they* will be screaming. I can't imagine a wider "we" versus "they" gulf than this.

Christians come across like: "The hour of decision is here. Won't you become a Christian today? You'll be eternally glad you did!" Why don't they just get to the point: "Join our club or burn, stupid."

Does Martin Zender fit this bill? I know that Jesus died for everyone, not just me ("God is the Savior of all humanity" 1

Timothy 4:10) . If it weren't for God giving me faith and a measure of morality in *this* life, I'd be another Hitler. Or a Mussolini. Or a Joel Osteen.

Score

Christianity: 6 Zender: 0

7. Financial involvement. *All or part of one's personal assets may be donated to the cult, increasing a vested interest in sticking with it and lessening the chance of returning to a former vocation.*

Does the Christian religion fit this bill? Hmm. Let me check.

Okay. I have just returned from a lengthy meeting with my fact checker (thank you, Ruth), and yes, it does appear that the Christian religion encourages the financial involvement of its members. (Much as a rolling truck tire encourages juice from a lemon.)

Benny Hinn (a famous Christian person in Florida), once suggested that, if Christians don't give enough money to finance evangelism, people will go to hell for eternity. How much money is enough? Call Benny, and he will be happy to define that term

for you, while sending you a deposit slip to his well-padded checking account.

Does Martin Zender fit this bill? I know this book costs money (about the same as a family-size pizza), but I'm not hanging over your shoulder bugging you to buy it. I hope I'm at home now, because that's where I like to be. I like the peace and quiet of my apartment. You stand alone with yourself, where you are. Bugging you for money is too much work, and I'm too lazy for it. You buy my book or you don't. God makes sure I have enough money to buy groceries and pay bills.

This charging you money for something is a new thing for me, anyway. It wasn't always this way.

I wrote a newsletter for seven years (in the '90s) and never charged anything for it. I just told people, "If this writing helps you, pay me what you think it's worth." For seven years, I supported my family of five by this method. I didn't work anywhere else on the side. I didn't deliver pizzas or run a paper route. I just studied Scripture, wrote about it, and mailed my newsletters.

Somebody once told me, "Do what you love, the money will come." I added to that ingredient a trust in God that bordered on the ridiculous. All my advertising came from people crying, "Yes!" at my newsletter, and then passing it on to others.

My wife stayed home with the kids, and I have three very fine children today.

Score
Christianity: 7 Zender: 0

8. Hypnotic states. *Inducing a highly susceptible state of mind may be accomplished by chanting, repetitious singing, or meditation.*

Does Christianity fit this bill? We already talked about this, Bob. But I will make this further observation: The Pentecostal-type people of the Christian religion do tend to chant like transcendentalists. I'm not condemning them, just observing. I have seen them in swoons. They raise their hands, glide back and forth, and say, "*Praise* You, Jesus, *praise* You, Jesus, *praise* You, Jesus," over and over again. They seem to be in some faraway land. It's breathy and yogi-like. They almost leave their bodies.

I'm all for praising Jesus. I like faraway lands. Yogis are good people. But what's with the swooning and the mantras? Does God want us to swoon? Does He ask us to chant? Find me one intelligent person of God in the Bible who did either thing. Yes, the people sang. Yes, they danced. Yes, they praised God. But they didn't black out their environment. You could have easily interrupted them for a cigarette. You can't interrupt a Pentecostal person today (especially not for a cigarette), not unless you want head-butted by a swoon.

Does Martin Zender fit this bill? Martin Zender begs you to keep your eyes and your mind open. Do not become cataleptic on me. I realize I'm quite handsome, but please do not swoon. The only thing that could make people susceptible to me is if God makes them naturally curious. Somebody once said I reminded them of the apostle Paul. Naturally, I was flattered. I said, "You mean my unswerving defense of the truth? My strong stance amid doctrinal chaos?"

"No," they said, "your expression is to be scorned." (From 2 Corinthians 10:10; I'm happy to be in Paul's company.)

Score:

Christianity: 8 Zender: 0

9. Isolation from outside. *Diminished perception of reality results when one is physically separated from friends, society, and the rational frame of reference in which one has previously functioned.*

Does Christianity fit this bill? Yes, especially in the "separated from the rational frame of reference" department. Why is it that, as soon as you enter the doors of a church, you have to leave your brain at the door? They should put up a sign beside four dozen large hooks:

HANG BRAIN HERE.

I have a friend who works for Motorola. He's a scientist and a mathematical wizard. His whole work is cause and effect: If he does *this*, then *this* will do *this*. His science is testable, rational, and true. Touch a wire, spark. Pour this here, smoke. One plus one plus one equals three.

Then he goes to church and all the rules change. There's a new frame of reference now: non-rational. The sign says (or should say): MOTOROLA MINDS DON'T WORK HERE.

In my friend's church, one plus one plus one equals one. He puts up no objection. It's a mystery, he's told, and he accepts that. *No objection, your honor. Can't explain it, but I don't need to.* ACCEPTABLE STUPIDITY, that's the creed here. Motorola would fire him for this. His church congratulates him. What's the deal? New frame of reference, that's what. New world, new rules.

This marks a cult.

Cause-and-effect need not apply in such an environment. God is in everything, but He doesn't affect people; they're free, so they say. Nothing causes them to act, nothing. God pushes the domino, the domino does not fall. It happens only in church. Very weird. *Push*, nothing. *Push*, nothing. It's anti-science.

Eat enough pies and cookies, and it probably won't bother you.

Does Martin Zender fit this bill? My spirituality carries a magnifying glass. "He who is spiritual is examining all" (1 Corinthians 2:15). Contrast this with *ignoring* all. One of my favorite verses is Romans 12:2—"Be transformed by the renewing of your mind." We're to be transformed by the renewing of our minds, then, not the removing of them.

Score
Christianity: 9 Zender: 0

10. Lack of privacy. *Reflective, critical thinking is impossible in a setting where cult members are seldom left unattended, and the ego's normal emotional defensive mechanisms can easily be stripped away by having the new member share personal secrets that can later be used for intimidation.*

Does Christianity fit this bill? I don't know. I'll ask the first unattended Christian I can find.

Someone sent me a brochure from the Springmill Church of God in Mansfield, Ohio. The brochure said: BE A PART OF OVER 70 EXCITING MINISTRIES. I was looking for the fine print that said and kiss your spare time good-bye, but it must have been too fine to see.

I know what you're thinking. You're thinking: *Come on, Martin. "Seventy exciting ministries" is a figure of speech. There can't be that many ministries in one church.* You're right. I only counted 66. Some of them I can't explain (Ark, Telecare, Battalion, F.T.H., Y.L.M., Joybelles, Fund Raising), but here they are anyway (Copied verbatim from the brochure. Who could make this up?):

FELLOWSHIP
Singles 1 (Flying Eagles)
Singles 2
Young Couples
Abundant Life (40's)
Senior Adult
Church Fellowship Events

MEN'S (Deacons)
Motorcycle Fellowship
D.A.D.S.
Men's Fellowship
Stevens (Helps)
Ushering
Greeting
Facility Stewardship
Grounds Stewardship
Operations/Inventory
Visitation (Unsaved Husbands)
Ark

MUSIC & WORSHIP
Praise Teams
Adult Choir
Ensembles
Worship Singers
Orchestra
Multi-Media

CARE & PRAYER
Watchcare
Tuesday Visitation
Telecare
Emergency Prayer Chain
Pastor's Prayer Hedge
Sunday Intercessors
Ladies Prayer Group

CHRISTIAN EDUCATION
School of the Spirit (Adult)
Sunday School

F.T.H.
Peer Counseling

LADIES
Fund Raising
Visitation (Hospital)
Kitchen Helps
Lydians
Spiritual Life
Nursery
Mary & Martha
Women Reaching Women
   (Fellowship)
M.O.P.S.
   (Mothers of Preschoolers)
Wives in Christ

YOUTH DEPARTMENT
F.T.H. Program
Y.L.M.
Jr. Y.L.M.
Battalion
Youth Choir

CHILDREN'S DEPT.
Children's Churches (4)
Stockade
Treeclimbers
Joybelles
Bluebelles
Children's Choir

OUTREACH
Men's & Ladies Jail Services
Prison Bible Studies
Nursing Homes
Visitation (Jail Follow-up)

AUXILIARY
Writer's Guild
Women United in Prayer
Drama Club
Book Store
Tape Ministry

ADMINISTRATION
Office Helps
Custodial Helps

* * *

Can you imagine me trying to get someone from the Springmill Church of God, who is a part of "70 exciting ministries," to reflect and think critically?

Zender: Hello, Susan. Let's reflect and think critically today.
Susan: What *is* today?
Zender: Monday.
Susan: Oh, I can't. I'm doing *Kitchen Helps* for the *Lydians*.

Then I train *Worship Singers* for the *Flying Eagles.*

Zender: What about later?

Susan: Kaleigh has *Joybelles*, and Junior's got *Motorcycle Fellowship.*

Zender: Tomorrow?

Susan: I'm trimming the *Pastor's Prayer Hedge.* Then *Wives in Christ* have *Jail Services* and the *Follow-Up.* In the afternoon, I weed for *Grounds Stewardship* until *Youth Choir* starts.

Zender: Doesn't *Pastor's Prayer Hedge* count for *Grounds Stewardship?*

Susan: Very funny, Martin. You know, you would really benefit from *Telecare.*

Zender: How about tomorrow night?

Susan: Oh! I've never heard of *Tomorrow Night?* Is that a new program?

Zender: No. I mean, tomorrow night, the *night.*

Susan: Can't. I do *Unsaved Husbands* for Stella.

Zender: I don't understand.

Susan: I promised God to get Al into *Ark.*

Zender: Oh! Are you the one who got Ian into *Inventory?*

Susan: No. I got Don into *D.A.D.S.* Ethel got Ian into *Inventory.* Gilda got Greg into *Greeting.*

Zender: What about Wednesday?

Susan: Wanda got *her* into *Watchcare.*

Zender: No. I mean, Wednesday, as in the day.

Susan: No can do. Stevie has *Treeclimbers.* Then *Writer's Guild* has me *Intercessoring* for the *Orchestra.*

Zender: So Thursday is ...

Susan: ... booked. It's an *Emergency Prayer Chain* so the *Drama Club* can help *Battalion* bring *Spiritual Life* to the *Nursery.*

Zender: And on Friday you ....

Susan: ... supervise the *Book Store* and *Fund Raise* for *M.O.P.S.*

Zender: I may benefit from *Telecare*, Susan, but you need peer counseling.

Susan: That's Saturday, after *F.T.H.*

Zender: Quick! Have you ever shared personal secrets with your many and constant Christian intimates that have later been used for intimidation?

Susan: No! Never! Uh, well, not very often.

Zender: Has your ego's normal emotional defensive mechanisms ever been stripped away by the sharing of these secrets?

Susan: I'm a big loser anyway, so what does it matter!

Does Martin Zender fit this bill? You are nearly to the end of this book, and not once have I asked you to share a personal secret with me. I assure you that stripping away anyone's normal emotional defensive mechanisms is always the furthest thing from my mind. If your emotional defensive mechanisms have somehow become stripped during the course of reading, you may return this book to your bookseller, who has been personally instructed to shake his head disbelievingly, apologize to you on my behalf, and offer you a free café latte.

Score

Christianity: 10 Zender: 0

11. Love-bombing. *Physical affection and constant contrived attention can give a false sense of camaraderie.*

Does Christianity fit this bill? Like a landslide. If you've ever walked into a church as a first time visitor, you know what I mean. You have never been so loved. Men jump up to pump your hand. Women kiss you on both cheeks. You have never seen so many teeth in your life. Some of the older people stare at you and pet your

"This new church tennis league is great, Ron. We haven't had to
think once about Sarah being burned in hell for eternity."

head. Only people who have won trips to Hong Kong from Bob
Barker have been happier than these people now loving you.

Now loving you. There's a big hint there. Because this situation
can quickly change. Like a real bomb dropped from a B-52, the
Love Bomb falls with purpose: It wants to wreck your little village.
That is, it wants to break down your defenses so you will join its
cause. If you do join its cause, all will be well. After you have been
scorched by the initial blast, you have only to endure the slow,
radiant kind of love that nods your way every Sunday morning or
hands you a napkin for your donut.

Of course, if you do not join the cause, the pilot and bombardier assemble for one last raid. This one flies over your house and goes BANG-BANG-BANG on your door.

You let them in, as a friend of mine did. They tell you how *glad* they were to have you at their church last Sunday, and how much the older folks want to pet you again. The woman, Gladys, looks at you like Bambi looked at Thumper just before the big fire. The man has a tear in his eye. He wants to get some guys together and shingle your roof: "By God, and I mean we'll do it *today*," says Jack with his hand on your shoulder. And you have to believe he would. You have to believe he'd have Ed and Roger and Bobby and Alan over before the end of the day and you'd be a Promise Keeper by midnight—a Promise Keeper with new shingles on the roof of your house.

Of course, if you still don't join the cause, you can shingle your own stupid roof—and don't look now, but here comes the raging inferno. Aw. Suddenly, you're lying there on a bed of combustible pine needles gasping for a donut, for a napkin, for a smile. Gladys and Jack look on from afar, from the big Home Depot in the sky.

You had your chance.

Does Martin Zender fit this bill? I don't even *like* you. Just kidding. I do like you. You have been very patient with me. Everyone has been very polite so far. But do I love you? In a broad sort of way, I suppose I do. But how can I love you, really? I don't know you that well. I cannot pet you. This is just me. I can't be that fake. When I know you, yes—then, perhaps, I can pet you. But not now.

Score
Christianity: 11 Zender: 0

12. Megacommunication. *Long, confusing lectures can be an effective tool if the inductee is bombarded with glib rhetoric and catch phrases.*

Does Christianity fit this bill? The Trinity Broadcasting Network has perfected this bill. If Christian television isn't loving you until your skull cracks, then it's bombarding you with glib rhetoric and catch phrases; rhetoric and phrases like, "praise the Lord," "get saved," "come to Jesus," "Holy Ghost revival," "hour of decision," "blessings from the throne," and "operators are standing by."

Megacommunication transcends televised pulpit lectures and may also include postcards from small-town churches.

When I worked for the postal service, there would always be dozens of postcards mailed by local churches on Monday morning after figuring out on Sunday night who hadn't come to church:

Dear **DAMON**, We missed you at Sunday School.

Dear **JOY**, Sure could have used you in the nursery.

Dear **MADELENE**, *Donut Ministry* was not the same without you.

Dear **MRS. DOTSON**, You were supposed to pet the new people yesterday! *Where were you?*

Dear **LARRY THE EX-USHER**, We hope you are recovering from whatever you better be dying from.

If you subject yourself to this kind of hyper-accountability, don't blame Martin Zender. Don't blame me when you can't take a break two Sundays straight without Doris from *Membership* whispering to Edna from *Accountability*: "Where's our *Backslider* stationery?"

Does Martin Zender fit this bill? No! How's that for glib rhetoric?

Score
Christianity: 12 Zender: 0

13. New Relationships. *Marriage to another cult member and the destruction of past family relationships integrates one fully into the cult "family."*

Does Christianity fit this bill? Yes, especially the Catholic branch. I have a friend whose mom (a Catholic) would have gladly eaten Spam on Good Friday rather than have her son marry a Protestant. But he married a Protestant anyway. My friend's mom crossed herself so fast, she broke her nose. Nothing has been the same ever since between my friend and his mother.

After she got her nose fixed, my friend's mom looked down it constantly at her daughter-in-law. It's sad, really. The kids were never baptized in the Catholic church, so that made matters worse. The kids are going to hell, guaranteed. I don't know why she bothers buying the kids presents for their birthdays and Christmas. It'll just make it harder for them when they're in hell, and the presents stop coming. Can you imagine? In hell, *and* the presents stop coming.

Although Catholics aren't supposed to get divorced, I know my friend's mom would like it if my friend divorced the Protestant and married a good Catholic girl. It wouldn't matter if the girl were a whore, a witch, or a baby-boiler, as long as she was Catholic.

Does Martin Zender fit this bill? No. Marry anybody you want.

Score
Christianity: 13 Zender: 0

14. Nonsensical activities. *Games and other activities with no apparent purpose leave one dependent upon a group or leader to give direction and order.*

Does Christianity fit this bill?

OMG. Years ago, my oldest son Gabe wanted to go to one of the local youth group meetings in our home town, at one of the fastest-growing churches in the state of Ohio, and possibly in the entire universe. Never would I have sent a child unprepared into the deadly web of ignorance that is Christian youth group. First, I taught my child to think. Then I armed him with knowledge. Next, I packed him with emergency insulin injections. Only then did he go to youth group, if he wanted to.

I admit that I fidgeted the whole time Gabe was gone. At last, Gabe's friend's dad brought him home.

I shined a light into his eyes and his pupils still contracted, thank God. I asked him what one plus one plus one was, and he said, "three." I called him, "Brother Gabe," and he looked at me like I was nuts. So far, so good. But there was something yellow on his shoes.

"We had an egg race, Dad."

It was the classic Christian relay: spoon in mouth, egg in spoon, pass the egg around, try not to drop it. Gabe's team didn't win, but he said it was fun.

"But they couldn't get me to do the M&M game, Dad. It was too stupid. Me and three other guys sat it out."

The main playing piece was a gigantic bowl of powdered sugar. Buried at the bottom of the bowl was a peanut M&M. Six people with their hands behind their backs jammed their faces simultaneously into the sugar to find the M&M. One child reportedly died in the melee, but no one could identify her.

"Then came the Vaseline game, Dad."

"An excellent lubricating product! Please explain, son!"

"It was a Vaseline and cotton ball relay. Each person puts Vaseline on their nose. The first person in the relay picks up a cotton ball with his nose and passes it down the line. You can't use your hands, of course."

"What did you learn about God through all this?"

"Nothing. But I have to tell you about the cross-dressing game."

"Please do!"

Cross-Dressing Game consisted of two teams of twelve—six pairs—which then raced toward suitcases filled with men's and women's outfits; each teammate put on one of the outfits over his/her clothes. It's all about speed, of course, and many teams are girl-girl, boy-boy, so boys are donning petticoats, girls are plunging into men's pajama bottoms. When the teammates are dressed, they grab their suitcase, run back to their team, remove the clothes, and stuff them back into the suitcase. Then the next pair of competitors grabs the suitcase, runs to the dressing area, withdraws the same clothes, zips, snaps, buttons for all they're worth, then runs.

Elephant Game.

This continues until the police arrive.

Of course, I could see what was happening through all of this, and so could Gabe. Once the kids were goofy, breathless, and coated with sugar, the teeny-bopper teachers could begin explaining to them what Satan uses his pointy tail for, and why they should join the church.

Writing about all this has felt very good to me, but I have peaked. My momentum is gone and your curiosity about nonsensical Christian activities is satisfied. How can I now write about The Incredible Food Race at the First Baptist Church in Ashland, Ohio? I'm spent. It's quite unfortunate, because The Race had everything: teenagers, fast cars, a citywide chase, cheating, law breaking, ten fast-food joints, pork rinds, out-of-window vomiting, and six bottles of Imodium A-D.

Maybe I'll put it in the movie.

I close with this note from Trinity Church in Lansing, Michigan:

"**Food, fun, fellowship, and friends** are the highlights of the student-led outreach event of Crosswalk on Sunday, May 17. This event with a Hawaiian theme will feature 'Capture the Coconut' and a great time for everyone. Cost is just $4.00. Please encourage your senior high student to be a part of it all!" (There was one bit of good news in the Trinity Church brochure, and I quote: "Increased resistance to the Christian Church in Northern India has recently been reported.")

Does Martin Zender fit this bill? Martin Zender encourages the normal use of eggs, M&Ms, spoons, petticoats, Vaseline, Jello, and coconuts.

Score
Christianity: 14 Zender: 0

15. Pavlovian control. *Behavior modification by alternating reward and punishment leads to confusion and dependency.*

Does Christianity fit this bill? Christians make you think that God is only really, truly happy with you if you attend church. Once you're tied by guilt to a Christian system, you are tested with various bells and whistles. When you've learned to drool on command, you're a wrist-tinkle away from organizing the next Jello Jamboree.

Does Martin Zender fit this bill? At the sound of the bell, you will no longer ask this question.

Seriously, now: I travel across the country, speaking to people who are in control of their own minds. They come voluntarily to hear me, not because I would do something bad to them if they don't. If people do depend on me, it is because I have consistently presented them with well-researched Scriptural information. They take my information, and go their way. Some of them take the time to thank me; I appreciate that. But if they don't thank me, I refuse to punish them. Were I inclined to bring *some* sort of wrath upon their heads, in order to cruelly confuse them, I would send them on a mission to read as many church signs as possible.

Score
Christianity: 15 Zender: 0

16. Peer pressure. *By exploiting one's desire for acceptance, doubts about cult practices can be overcome by offering a sense of belonging to an affirming community.*

Does Christianity fit this bill? If church signs mean anything, yes. A church sign at the Baptist church back in Ohio says: WE WANT OUR CHURCH TO BE YOUR HOME.

This theme gushes from church signs everywhere. Spinning

yellow daisies capture the human soul. The church wants to be your all. Come and belong. Everything will be all right in your new family. You need to be loved, and they have love. You have emotional holes, and they have every brand of sugar-and-chemical filling.

We can measure Bob Larson's blindness on page 15 by the fact that he never looks up in a fit of revelation from the middle of any of his sentences to exclaim: "Oh, my God ..." No, Larson never sees the mutant camel bounding across his own page:

> Loneliness, indecision, despair, and disappointment are the emotional characteristics cult recruiters notice. They approach the unwary with an excessively friendly invitation to a lecture, free meal, weekend workshop, or other activity offering instant solutions to overwhelming problems. Surprisingly enough, few potential cultists bother to inquire about who is extending the offer, what is behind it, and what functions will take place. Vague answers are seldom challenged, leaving the recruiter an unassailable opportunity to obscure his intentions.

> Cults generally attract prospects with an outpouring of attention and affection, the so-called "love-bombing" technique. Feeling, not doctrine, is the lure. In fact, the belief structure is seldom mentioned in the beginning. Cult leaders know that once an initiate has been reconditioned to accept their particular worldview, and as soon as he feels a sense of meaningful belonging, his mind will be ready to accept any teaching, including a belief that the leader represents God.

> Approval, acceptance, belonging, authority—all those things that were missing are supplied by the cult. Motivation is generated by rewards for excessive zeal. Critical thinking

is discouraged and corporate identification with some larger-than-life mission (as conveyed by the leader) causes the member to equate what is good for the cult as being good for him.

When the recruit's mind shifts into neutral, the period of intensive indoctrination begins. The effectiveness of this tactic is often enhanced by sensory deprivation, extreme amounts of physical activity coupled with fatigue, severance of all ties with family and friends, and the forsaking of all belongings and material possessions. In a short time, the initiate becomes emotionally and spiritually dependent on the cult for decisions, direction, and even the physical necessities of life. The outside world appears more and more threatening. Finally his mind "snaps," and "the sudden, drastic alteration of personality in all its many forms" takes place.

NOTE FROM MARTIN: What does it mean to be institution-alized? We get a good answer from an unexpected source: a man named "Red" in the movie *The Shawshank Redemption*. Morgan Freeman plays Red, who is serving a life sentence for murder. One of his fellow cons, an old man named Brooks (James Whitmore) finally gets paroled after decades in the pen. Brooks, however, is having trouble on the outside; he can't adjust to freedom. Brooks sends the gang a postcard; he's depressed and suicidal. No one can figure it out except Red. Sitting in the prison yard one day, Red explains that Brooks had become institutionalized. Fifty years in the pen, said Red, and the institution was all he knew. Inside, he was an important man. Outside, he felt lost. He couldn't cope on his own. Red paused to scan the walls. First a man hates these walls, he said. Then he gets used to them. If enough time passes, a man comes to depend on them. "That," said Red, "is institutionalized."

Does Martin Zender fit this bill? I have nothing for you to join. I like you, but I don't have either the time or the desire to be your "affirming community." I am no one's "go to" guy for spirituality. I will continue to write books that will help deliver you from religious bondage and give you peace, but I cannot *personally* help you. Don't depend on me. I'm a working-class writer, not a guru. I'm too lazy to run a cult. I can't afford to offer you a free meal. I *could* be excessively friendly, but I find it easier to sit at home and watch a movie. I like being appreciated and respected, as long as it happens from ten miles away.

Go directly to God with your needs. Depend on Him. Pour out your soul to God. Gather with friends who also believe in the one true God.

Score
Christianity: 16 Zender: 0

17. Sensory deprivation. *Fatigue coupled with prolonged activity can make one vulnerable to otherwise offensive beliefs and suggestions.*

Does Christianity fit this bill? Eternal torment is the most offensive doctrine ever. *Ever.* We've already looked at some of the many stupid church activities that numb people's minds and shift them to neutral. Such shifting makes the mind say: "I can now receive the unreceivable."

Otherwise known as brainwashing.

Eternal torment is the unreceivable. That so many Christians have received it is proof of brainwashing. That so many Christians so casually accept it as the fate of most of humanity is proof of an altered mind. That so many Christians think endless torture is a fitting end to "God's great plan of salvation" proves that Christianity is the most mind-altering drug on the face of the earth.

The doctrine of eternal torment is not a Scriptural doctrine. That doctrine was invented when the King James and other versions unaccountably put "eternal" and "everlasting" (for the Greek adjective *aionion,* which always has to do with time) to describe the chastisement of unbelievers; suddenly, a false Scriptural veneer was lent to an otherwise insane concept. (This translation problem is similar to the one that made *ekklesia* "church" in one place, and "assembly" in another.)

The *King James Version* and others (like the *New International Version*) also mislead people by translating three different Greek words (*hades, gehenna,* and *tartarus*), with the same English word, "hell." The next time a KJV or NIV person tells you to go to hell, ask him which one you should go to. Neither *hades, gehenna,* nor *tartarus* have anything to do with the traditional Christian concept of a place where your unbelieving family members will be tormented in flame forever. In a correctly translated Bible (such as the *Concordant Literal New Testament, Young's Literal New Testament,* or *The Emphasized Bible*), the doctrine of eternal torment disappears. There are still plenty of judgments in Scripture, but none of them are eternal. Eternal judgment is a ridiculous concept. God's judgments lead someplace. Always. They are processes, not goals.

Back in 1999, I went on the air in Cleveland with five other friends. We did a live, call-in radio show two hours a night, five nights a week, for five weeks. We called our show *Grace Café.* As we became sufficiently bold, we decided to commit one of those weeks to refuting eternal torment. We called it "Hell Week."

You've got to understand how bizarre this was. We were in a Christian studio undoing everything Christians believed in. The only reason we got in was because Denise Telep, the woman who landed us the contract, didn't quite tell them everything. She only said, "We're going to be controversial." The station managers said,

"Okay, that's good. Controversy makes good radio."

Isn't that a fact.

I remember sitting in Talk Studio B on the first day of Hell Week, looking out the glass at pictures of Billy Graham, James Dobson, Charles Stanley, and other pillars of the Christian religion. I remember thinking, *Well, they're never going to put up our pictures on this wall, but we're going to rock this town with truth.*

We covered every angle of eternal torment known to humans. It was one of the most exhausting weeks of my life. Every door we went through, we slammed shut with Scripture. No one could convict us on Scriptural grounds. They could hate our guts and call us names (which some callers did, including "*Universalists!*" and

Grace Café Radio. WCCD 1100 AM
Cleveland, Ohio; August, 1999
(That's me in back with the coffee mug.)

"*Unitarians!*" none of which we are), but they couldn't prove us wrong. We were broadcasting to a potential listening audience of over two million people. We knew that Christian pastors and teachers were listening to the show. We heard through some of our friends (friends who had also left the church) that some pastors were telling their congregations not to listen to us. Naturally, all these people were listening their brains out.

I remember challenging the pastors and teachers on the air: "It is your responsibility to keep your flocks in darkness. It is your sworn duty to protect your people from truth. If what we're teaching is wrong, it is your solemn responsibility to call us right now, on the air, and tell us we're wrong. (I gave the number.) Then tell us *why* we're wrong. Show us the Scriptures that *prove* we're wrong. If you don't call to straighten us out, we'll consider it a tacit admission that everything we're teaching is right."

I was on a roll and went on like that for some time.

Not one working pastor or teacher called our show that week. It wasn't that they didn't hate us. They did. It wasn't that they weren't listening. They were. It was because we twisted every screw down so tightly that none of them could move. There was not a

Hell week.

professional pastor or teacher in the city of Cleveland who felt like being embarrassed on live radio by a half dozen broadcasting amateurs opening Pepsi cans on the air, who happened also to have one-hundred years of independent Scripture study between them, and Scriptural backup for everything they said.

I'm saying all this now, at the end of the book, because it's frustrating for me, at this point, to not be able to satisfy every objection or question coursing through the minds of the troubled and near-rejoicing. Those details will take another book. (And what do you know; I've written one. Please see my book, *Martin Zender Goes to Hell*.) But know this: There *are* answers. These brief paragraphs are for those who now suffer emotionally and spiritually from the false teaching of eternal torment. They are for those who have lost unbelieving loved ones, or who now have children who are rebelling against God and mired in every kind of sin. They are for those fearful for their own salvation. These people, whom I truly care for and want to help, must not leave this book without knowing for certain that God is good. They have not received that assurance in church.

God will exceed, not dash, your highest expectations. God is not crazy; He is not cruel. He does judge, yes, but He judges righteously. His righteous judgments never exceed His love. He judges in love. Love oversees and tempers all that God does; God *is* love.

God's love conquers all. You have always known that, but perhaps you have let other people talk you out of it. Like my friend Steve, whom I will talk about soon, perhaps you have been persuaded that *you* are the crazy one for thinking that God must be better than the clergy say He is. But deep down, you have held out for truth—and now you know it. Now you can add this wonderful bit of information to your spiritual gut-knowledge:

Scripture has been on your side all along.

The salvation of all is the only outcome worthy of God. Many do believe this in their hearts, but are afraid to say it. Most don't realize that Scripture supports it. When translated rightly, Scripture more than supports it. Scripture *teaches* it. "God is the Savior of all humanity, especially of believers." *Especially* of believers, not exclusively of them. God gives belief to some people now; He gives belief to the rest later. Some come early, some come late—but all come. That was 1 Timothy 4:10, just quoted. (Look it up in any version.) It's only one verse. There are others. Like 1 Corinthians 15:22 and Romans 5:18. And 1 Timothy 2:6—the return of all to God happens in due time, "in its own eras." Jesus' suffering on the cross is the basis for this blessing. Remember the first thing I asked God to show me over thirty years ago: *What happened at the cross?*

He has shown me, and not only me. Many revel in this, one of the greatest truths in Scripture.

This news ought to relieve any closet believers who are reading. If more people knew that Scripture supported them in their gut feelings about God, they'd be bold. They would jump up and shout above the din of the crowd: "God is good!" Everything that came out of God returns to God— read Romans 11:36 and Colossians 1:16-20—eventually. This lifetime does not empty God's storehouse of grace. The return of all creation to its Creator is not the wishful thinking of teary-eyed grandmothers. It's the unmistakable testimony of rightly translated Scripture.

Therefore, as far as making people vulnerable to otherwise offensive beliefs and suggestions: Does Martin Zender fit this bill? *No. His news is too good.*

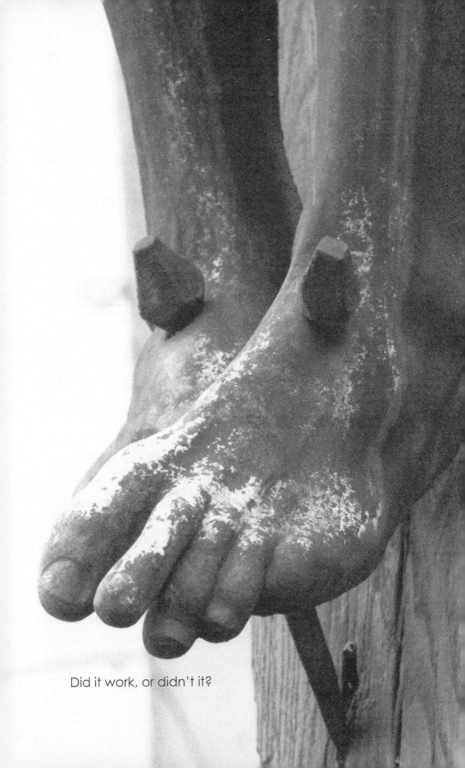

Did it work, or didn't it?

Score
Christianity: 17 Zender: 0

18. Unquestioning submission. *Acceptance of cult practices is achieved by discouraging any questions or natural curiosity that may challenge what the leaders propagate.*

Does Christianity fit this bill? Yes, and Steve will now tell you about it.

We had dinner and an impromptu talk about God last Saturday night with Steve, his wife, and another couple.

Steve's wife Sheila had dragged him to church five years ago. Steve kicked and screamed like the trooper that he is, but off he went for the sake of his wife.

Steve still had his own brain then, so he resisted every contradiction the church threw up against him. Steve asked normal questions, which naturally irritated the leaders. *Why couldn't Steve just shut up?* Sheila kicked her poor husband's shins repeatedly in that church.

A year passed.

"They eventually broke me," Steve said. "It took about a year, but they finally convinced me that *I* was the one from Mars—that *I* was the one who had everything messed up. Now I'm starting to realize I had everything right and *they* were from Mars, which kind of irritates me. It makes me wonder why I had to go through all that."

(Sheila hid her head in her hands.)

"I'm not saying I had everything figured out," continued Steve, "but at least I was asking the right questions. My natural questions *were* the right questions, but these were the questions that made everybody nervous. It took them a year to institutionalize me, but they finally did it. I was outnumbered. I finally figured that with so many people against me, I *had* to be wrong. I didn't know then that in the Bible, the religious majority were always the wrong ones. I didn't know there was such a strong precedent for that in my favor. I wish I knew then that the Bible was on my side. But the church finally shoved their brand of tinted glasses on my face that made me see everything their way. Now I have to admit it's a bit of a struggle to see things the other way, the right way."

Sheila is embarrassed about dragging Steve to church. Now she feels she hurt him unnecessarily and delayed their spiritual progress. Of course, she did what she thought was best. She thought Steve would go to hell if he didn't go to church and hear a "salvation message."

After five years of church, Steve is hearing a salvation message for the first time in his life. Blood is slowly returning to his cerebrum.

Does Martin Zender fit this bill? You already know. I encourage people to ask questions. I answer their questions to the best of my knowledge, and then I tell them, "Don't believe this because *I'm* telling you; be like the noble Bereans (Acts 17:11) and search the Scriptures yourselves to see if what I'm telling you is true." I only have one more point and I want to get it over with. By the way:

Score
Christianity: 18 Zender: 0

19. Value rejection. *As the recruit becomes more integrated into the cult, he is encouraged to denounce the values and beliefs of his former life.*

Does Christianity fit this bill? Before becoming Christians, people hear about eternal torment and are horrified. It repulses them. They can't believe that the almighty, loving God would do something to His children that not even they—weak and sinful humans—would dream of doing to theirs, not even if they hated them. This shows good values.

But after becoming Christians, these same people are brainwashed into thinking that eternal torment now somehow illustrates God's perfect love. When a non-initiated person asks one of those dumb questions like, "How can eternal torment possibly illustrate the love of God?" the Christian answers, "Well, God's love is not like our love, you see."

So the pre-Christian's concept of love changes radically upon becoming Christianized, which explains why Christians, throughout history, have been such ferocious warriors and torture-mongers. Why should they be more loving than their Deity? The human value system (where love is love) has been traded for the imagined Divine value system (where love includes pitiless torture).

The following is excerpted from *Sismondi's History of Crusades Against the Albigenes*, chap. ii 73–84, & c:

> The more zealous, therefore, the multitude were for the glory of God, the more ardently they labored for the destruction of heretics, the better Christians they thought themselves. And if at any time they felt a movement of pity or terror, whilst assisting at their punishment, they thought it a revolt of the flesh, which they confessed at the tribunal of penitence; nor could they get quit of their remorse till their priests had given them absolution.

> Amongst them all not a heart could be found accessible to pity. Equally inspired by fanaticism and the love of war, they believed that the sure way to salvation was through the field of carnage. Seven bishops, who followed the army,

had blessed their standards and their arms, and would be engaged in prayer for them while they were attacking the heretics. Thus did they advance, indifferent whether to victory or martyrdom, certain that either would issue in the reward which God himself had destined for them.

Does Martin Zender fit this bill? I forgive you for even asking. If your former beliefs were wrong, then go ahead and denounce the beliefs of your former life. The familial values of love, however, are timeless; these I always encourage.

A mother's love for her child, for instance, illustrates God's love; same with a father's love for his son. God gave us these pictures to teach us about *His* love. I'd like to ask this of hard-core Christians: Are we supposed to believe that God's love is reflected in a mother's affection for her child in this lifetime only? Are you telling us that, in God's program of progressive revelation, the whole concept of love changes from that which we've known? I could see it if the love became better and wider as we moved on toward God. But you're telling us that it degenerates as the picture lifts higher?

I think not.

Final Score
Christianity: 19 Zender: 0
So is Christianity a cult or is Martin Zender a cult? Use your own brain. I refuse to tell you anything.

Some Christians—Bono of U2, for instance—are philanthropists. The world is a better place, physically, because of them. The hungry have food and the homeless have homes. In light of this, we are tempted to overlook Christianity's doctrinal flaws. Should we, however, use her social heroics to shield her from the crime of distorting the true gospel? As long as a cult gives shoes to the poor, can't we excuse it for making salvation come through human decision, rather than through Christ? Can't good people be forgiven, even if they do teach doctrines of demons such as eternal torment?

Absolutely not! Says Bob Larson:

> Do false belief systems deserve credit for their good works? Many cults have made significant contributions to the social welfare of humanity. In some instances cult leaders are sincerely concerned about meeting the spiritual needs of seeking souls. Even though this book recognizes positive elements in certain cults, it must not be forgotten that the Bible requires reproof and rebuke of any teaching that exalts itself against the necessity of salvation through Christ (2 Timothy 4:2). According to Scriptural criteria, any false teacher is a "deceitful Christ" (Philippians 3:18). Gratuitous words in recognition of positive values should not be mistaken for any endorsement of what the Bible calls "doctrines of devils" (1 Timothy 4:1).
>
> The good works and apparent beneficial effects of a cult's belief system thus are inconsequential considerations (Pg. 20).

8.
THERE'S NO PLACE LIKE HOME

THERE'S NO PLACE LIKE HOME

I still study Scripture on my own, as I have done for thirty-five years now. I still don't go to church. I meet with friends in homes, in parking lots, or under evergreen trees—wherever God deems fit.

We have regular Bible studies where I live now. One person may start things off, but everyone participates. This is a beautiful thing because of how freelance it is. There is no set agenda here, and no real schedule. Everything just goes like it's supposed to go. Different people come all the time.

We talk about anything and everything. No subject is taboo. No one says, "Oh, we shouldn't talk about that," or "That's a ridiculous and embarrassing question, Carol." No. Everything is honest and open. Our conversation flows like a river where everyone gets splashed.

This could be the best Bible study ever. There is knowledge and understanding here. Four of the most spiritual words I have ever heard are: "Oh, I get it." A lot of that goes on here, and I know it is going on in different places across the country.

We've never been on Christian television, in case you haven't deduced that.

So that's what I'm doing now: meeting and studying with believers. And of course, I'm still traveling, speaking at conferences, writing, recording my daily audio show, and making videos.

I like to go where there are seeking and open-minded people. I gather with new folks whenever God gives the opportunity. In other words, I am always willing to travel in order to speak about God. God orchestrates everything in the manner of a choreographer.

I am in a ballet where all the people are dancing.

9.

EPILOGUE: NOW WHAT?

EPILOGUE: NOW WHAT?

The world turns from God because it thinks God is a monster and a hypocrite. The world did not get this idea on its own: The Christian religion taught it.

The church spends millions of dollars fighting monsters it spends millions of dollars creating and feeding. Nothing that Christianity can say will move the world toward righteousness. No, wait. It's worse. The more renowned Christian leaders speak, the farther the world moves *from* righteousness.

I say: Believe in God, no matter *what* the clergy tell you.

The church fails to grasp that its foundation is skewed. The foundation I speak of is the church's conception of God: it is diametrically opposed to truth. Everything the church builds upon this foundation, therefore, is doomed—to say the least. No one in the Christian movement realizes this. They are all trying to patch surface cracks, never suspecting that the source of trouble lies in their own bedrock.

Only when the world sees the true God (or at least rids itself of the Christian one), will it right itself morally. The tree with the most light produces the most fruit. You can curse all you want at a tree in darkness; it won't produce. Put the tree in sunlight (or take away the buildings that keep it in shade), and then sit in a lawn chair and watch; the fruit takes care of itself.

As I told you in the last chapter, I wrote a newsletter for seven years in the '90s. The soulish appeal of it (I was embarrassed to discover) was its amateurish sincerity. The intellectual appeal was its information, which was clear and verifiable. I never asked anyone to believe *me*. Rather, I gave my readers evidence. My cartoons appealed to those like me with a quirky sense of humor. An easily detected spiritual substance undergirded the whole, as the newsletters got passed to grandmothers as well as teenagers, scientists as well as college dropouts, clergymen as well as criminals, all of whom rejoiced in God, not Martin Zender.

Each edition of that newsletter took on a life of its own.

How to explain it? The Spirit of God, first. Secondly, I was a maverick. I did not have to answer to a church board or toe a denominational line; people liked that. I could write about what I saw in Scripture without worrying about censure from "higher ups." My only higher-up was God. People paid me to be a maverick. They valued my system-less existence. They sent me money to make sure I never did anything for money. Does that make sense?

I became acquainted with many people through that simple, eight-page publication, most of whom I have never met—but I knew them just the same. During some point in their lives, every one of these people had cried out to God, as I had: *I have to know You, I have to know You, I have to know You.*

Now that you have finished this book and have taken it to

heart, you may be asking, "What do I do now?" You're in the same strange place I was nearly forty years ago, wanting to seek God and fellowship with other people, but realizing more than ever that the religious establishment hurts rather than helps.

I have come up with a solution that may work for you.

The greatest thing about the early church was its spontaneity and loose structure. That kind of freedom is most closely imitated today by home gatherings. I enjoy the meetings I attend here in Pennsylvania for the reasons already mentioned. My thought was, since I know so many people around the country who have enjoyed my work and the work of those like me, why not connect these folks with others seeking fellowship?

My friend Clyde L. Pilkington, Jr. of Study Shelf Books in Pennsylvania has created a feature on his website for this purpose, and I have linked to it from my own site. Go to www.martinzender. com, click the "Meet Other People" tab on my home page, and it will take you to Clyde's feature. Then, click on your home state. There, you will find a list of people in your area who would love to meet you, or who are at least willing to hear from you and/or fellowship. If there is no one in your state, sign in and be the first. If there are enough people in an area—who knows? Maybe you could start your own home-based Bible study.

The one thing these people have in common is that they are all true seekers who value Scripture and recognize Jesus Christ as God's Son. In some way or another, all have sampled and rejected the religious institutions of humans, and found them wanting.

As long as you're at my website, take a thorough look around. You will find many writings, audio teachings, radio broadcasts, and videos—hours of free material at your disposal. I am known as "The World's Most Outspoken Bible Scholar"—for a reason. This warning appears on my home page:

WARNING! You have reached the home of **"The World's Most Outspoken Bible Scholar."** This website may cause excitability in professional theologians and seminary students. **Adults and children 12 years of age and older:** Do not browse this website for more than five minutes at a time. At higher doses, unbearable relief may occur. **Avoid operating a motor vehicle while browsing this site.** If you are pregnant or nursing a theological bias, please consult your physician. A persistent reliance on orthodox tradition may be sign of a serious condition. In case of overdose, start singing a loud, happy song. Laugh.

Looking forward to seeing you down the road.

Grace and peace,
Martin

For further information:
www.martinzender.com
www.concordant.org
www.studyshelf.com
www.sheridanvoice.com

Additional books by Martin Zender:

Flawed by Design
The First Idiot in Heaven
Martin Zender Goes to Hell
Clanging Gong News Collector's Edition
How to be Free From Sin While Smoking a Cigarette
Martin Zender's Guide to Intelligent Prayer
The Really Bad Thing About Free Will

 www.facebook.com/zendermeister

"God used this small book to change my life. After fifteen years in the pulpit, I finally understand what hell is. Better late than never."

-J. Marcus Oglesby, M.Div.

MARTIN ZENDER
GOES TO HELL

MARTIN ZENDER
Author of "How to Quit Church Without Quitting God"

At last. Here are the facts.

EXCERPT
MARTIN ZENDER GOES TO HELL

When Adam sinned, what was the consequence? Go and
see. Here was the worst sin ever. What better time to
reveal the ultimate, horrible fate? But it's not there. You'll be driven
from the Garden, Adam, and you'll have to hoe like mad to make
anything grow. Eve, childbearing will introduce you to pain so severe
you'll see white. And today, you begin to die, both of you. It's the
penalty of your disobedience. Death and weeds and cramps the color
of lightning. And I should mention this as well—I won't be coming
around as often.

Bad enough, but not a word about an eternity of torture in flames.
I wonder why. Do you?

Along comes Cain then, who murders his brother Abel. Murder
is an unknown crime until then, but the worst since the Satan/Eve/
fruit debacle. Now is a good time for God to unveil the Mother of
All Punishments, to discourage future lawbreakers. But no, not a
word about it. There is judgment, yes, but it's rational and reason-
able: Cain's farming labors get cursed—the ground won't produce
for him—and he has to wander the Earth as a nomad. We anticipate
such phrases as, "Burn forever, murderer," or, "Go to hell, Cain," but
they are not here.

I hope no one is disappointed.

What about in the days of Noah? The citizens of that era sinned
as a profession. All people thought about back then was: How can
we sin with more skill and greater efficiency? They loved their grim
occupation and rarely took a break from it. If any people deserved

eternal torment, it was these. Burn the blasphemers in hell forever? Surprisingly, no. The sinners merely got wiped out in a flood. Merely? Think about it. One glug and down came your curtain. It couldn't have been pleasant, but it was better than burning forever.

God does sometimes employ fire and brimstone to curtail the careers of professional sinners. Like Lysol, however, fire and brimstone kill germs on contact. (That is, the fire and brimstone do not eternally torment the germs.) Consider the twin cities of Sodom and Gomorrah, cities which today have become synonymous with sexual perversion. When the hour of reckoning arrived, "The Lord rained on Sodom and Gomorrah brimstone and fire from the Lord out of heaven" (Genesis 19:24). The result? God "destroyed the cities of the valley" (verse 29). Note the conspicuous absence of "God began to torment the inhabitants of these cities for eternity."

What about in the days of Moses, when there were laws for everything and a thousand ways to break them? Here's another ideal opportunity for the doctrine of eternal torment to begin "crawling all over Scripture," as I've been told that it is. And yet, it is another opportunity squandered by God and His servant Moses, who could get mad enough to smash rock. All threats in the days of Moses concerned earthly rewards and punishments only. Kill another man's bull, and your bull was killed. Mishandle some point of law, and your crops failed. Tangle with Moses himself, and some terrible thing happened with your wife's hormones. Or an enemy would storm your gates. Or both.

All bad enough, but not crazy. Nothing eternal and not a hint of unending flame. Capital punishment was by stoning then, the worst that could happen. It was nothing you wanted in on, but at least you died. One rock to the head relaxed you enough to dim the finish. No more taxes, tents, scorpions, sand storms, or Moses. For men and women toiling and failing upon an evil planet, death often came as a mercy.

To review, nowhere in the Old Testament does any God-inspired writer mention one word about an eternity of torment for disobeying God. Not one scholar has ever found it, no, not even those who have searched for it desperately. Strange that a doctrine that is "everywhere" has not yet appeared in a segment of the Bible that is, by my reckoning, about three and a half inches thick.

Is it that the amateurs of that delicate era could not shoulder such a responsibility? Then let the Old Testament lightweights stand aside to make way for Someone Who Knows How To Damn. Close the Old Testament books, and make way for genuine terror. Turn one page past Malachi, all ye sinners. To the Gospels! But rejoice not. Rather, fear. For you did not realize how good you had it in the days of old. You are about to pine for those days of flood, famine, and stone. For here, finally, comes One Rising to New Levels of Damnation, a Divine Unveiler of Heretofore Unimaginable Torture. His Good News, in a nutshell, is "Love Me before you die, or my Father will do worse than kill you!" His name?

JESUS CHRIST, SAVIOR.

The spirit of the Lord is on Me, on account of which He anoints Me to bring the evangel to the poor. He has commissioned Me to heal the crushed heart, to herald to captives a pardon, and to the blind the receiving of sight; to dispatch the oppressed with a pardon, to herald an acceptable year of the Lord...
—Jesus Christ, Luke 4:18-19

Are you ready now to find out how things *really* are?

Pages 35-38

The most frightening threats Jesus made to the Israelites are probably those found in Matthew 5:29-30 and Mark 9:43-48. Here, Jesus explains how much better it is for an Israelite to pluck out his or her eye, or tear off his or her hand, than to let these members lead one into "the fire of hell." These verses have terrified countless millions over the centuries, people to whom the verses don't even apply. These are Israelite threats for an earthly, Israelite kingdom.

The "fire of hell"? That's bad translating. Jesus never said the word "hell" in His life. He didn't speak English. The word that left His lips was *Gehenna*. That's right. Jesus warned the Israelites about "the fire of Gehenna," not hell, and any concordance will confirm this for you (see word #1067 in Strong's, and page 474 in Young's.) Gehenna is a small valley along the southwest corner of Jerusalem. It's a geographical location, a place you can walk in today. God made sure that some versions of Scripture got this right (the *Concordant Literal New Testament, Rotherham's Emphasized Bible*, and *Young's Literal Translation*, to name three).

As any dictionary will tell you, Gehenna is where the Israelites of old dumped their garbage and offered sacrifices to foreign gods. In the old days it was called the Valley of Hinnom. From *The Random House Dictionary*, under the entry *Gehenna*: "The valley of Hinnom, near Jerusalem, where propitiatory sacrifices were made to Molech." It may be a pleasant green valley today, but in the 1,000-year kingdom it will function as a crematorium for the corpses of criminals (Isaiah 66:23-24).

The "fire of hell"? Here is the only instance where the *King James Version* has taken the name of an actual place and made it something else. Watch this: Where the Greek has *Hierousalem*, the KJV translates "Jerusalem"—every time. Where the Greek has *Nazaret*, the KJV makes it "Nazareth"—every time. Where the Greek has *Bethleem*, the KJV has "Bethlehem"—every time. This is sensible. It's an honorable and consistent way of translating. But here, where Jesus says *Gehenna* (another geographical location), the KJV (as well as the *New International Version*—NIV—and *New American Standard Bible*—NASB), makes it "hell." Gee, that's weird. Can you explain it? I can. Ever hear the phrase, "theological bias"?

Pages 43-46

Matthew, chapter 25. Here we find "the Son of Mankind come into His glory, seated on the throne." In front of Him are gathered "all the nations," and "He shall be severing them from one another even as a shepherd is severing the sheep from the goats." This judgment is advertised in your local church as "the final judgment" of "all humankind," when "God's enemies" go to either "heaven or hell," for "all eternity." But no. Each sheep and goat represents a nation, not a person. This is not Uncle Harry standing before Jesus; it is Ethiopia. It is not Aunt Hazel trembling before Him; it is Russia. It is not Jim the milkman; it is Afghanistan.

This judgment occurs at the inauguration of the thousand-year kingdom, in the valley of Jehoshaphat. Like Gehenna, this is a literal, geographical location outside Jerusalem (see map again on page 37). As with Gehenna's fire and worms, this judgment is practical. Jesus returns to find Earth's political alignments amok. Good nations will be low; the evil will sit on high. The Great Judge will cure this. What criteria will He use for judging? Their belief in Him? Their confession of faith? The mode of their baptism? No. It will be that nation's policy toward Israel, nothing more. No one will ask, "What church did you go to?" or, "Why didn't you have more faith?"

To make this the general judgment of all humanity is to slaughter the context. But who cares? The possibility of a near-universal twisting of this judgment, and a vast misrepresentation of God's character, will not bother most people. Why? I will tell you. ■

Dear Martin,
I have just finished *Martin Zender Goes to Hell*. This is one of the best books I have ever read. All anxiety over my loved ones has vanished. Praise God! The facts you present are unassailable. —*Stephen S.*

What if God made you the way you are on purpose?

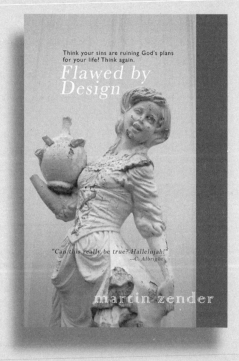

Think your sins are ruining God's plans
for your life? Think again.

Flawed by Design

"Can this really be true? Hallelujah!"
—C. Albright

martin zender

Flawed by Design

EXCERPT
FLAWED BY DESIGN

Pages 11-13

A woman crashes into the home of Simon the Pharisee. The town sinner, she neither knocks nor removes her sandals. Whoredom is fresh on her clothes, yet something belying this rests angelically upon her face. Only one person here can appreciate the transformation. The woman hurries to the feet of the Master.

An unusual thing had occurred in the early morning hours of that day, after the last man (the last client) had slipped into the Jerusalem night. As she looked about her cubicle, a dread of the future gripped her. Why should she feel this now? Why tonight? No immediate answer came, yet a vision of her final hours flickered in the flame of her one remaining candle. She would die in this room; which night, she did not know. It would be soon, though. Death would come slowly in a pool of blood, released onto the floor by her own hand. Her sister Mariba would find her. Mariba would scream, there would be a funeral—thirty days of mourning—then it would all be over.

The walls closed in. Stars twinkled outside these walls, somewhere. A sun shone on the other side of Earth, though not for her. For her there was only the shadow cast by her burning piece of wax, a leather ghost running from her feet to a corner, up a wall, across the ceiling, then back to her naked feet. Nothing could escape the cubicle. Floor, wall, ceiling, then back to engulf her. Her hands went to her face now; she was crying.

She had to get out.

Not one other soul occupied the side street where she burst from her home. Urgency along this void of humanity became her silent scream. She would not break down in the city.

Outside the Essene gate, down the valley of Hinnom, up over the aqueduct, then west toward the Bethlehem Road; this brought her to the field. Recently gleaned, dead and quiet, the soil sent coolness into her legs. From above, the heavens lay frozen and mute. Between these two voids she fell to her knees to gather a piece of Earth. Instead, she found a stone, for God had placed it there centuries ago, for her to find. Now it would become her means of hating Him. She picked up the stone as a man would grasp it, then found her feet. Her left eye was already trained into the heavens, right wrist cocked toward the throne room.

All agonies now shifted to the act of throwing. Every sinew, muscle, joint, and fragment of despair made ready the rock for the face of God. She would hit Him, yes. And her tongue, too, lay poised with the forbidden question, "What have You *made* me?!"

The stone traveled a little way into space, propelled by the impetus of the word "made." But then it returned to Earth, though she never heard where.

She had missed.

The forbidden question, however, had not missed at all. In fact, it had hit squarely, and she knew it. Something had happened. Now she felt millions of invisible eyes. She had unmistakably commanded something, perhaps everything. The field was now a stage. With knowledge of this came a liberating rush of boldness. What happened next happened too quickly to stop.

❦

Pages 29-30

Frustrated with your failures? Feeling condemned? Can't overcome a bad habit? I've got great news for you:

"Now we have this treasure in earthen vessels, that the transcendence of the power may be of God and not of us" (2 Corinthians 4:7).

Your humble little vessel of sin is made that way on purpose. We are clay pots by design, not because we have gone afoul of God's intention for us. Let this revelation soothe the exhausted self-improver. Retire, Christian soldier! You fail by design, not because you are a failure. God wants you cognizant of the source of your power, and He has many creative ways of driving this home. One of these is sin.

Wouldn't some of us love to shed our earthenware now and still walk among mortals? Our sins keep us from producing a perfect walk, and we mourn this. What we do not understand is that an imperfect walk is the main idea of this life. God puts the treasure of His spirit in earthen vessels now to keep the vessels from situating themselves upon high places. A perfect walk is not what we need right now. Who could live with us? Could we stand ourselves? Humility is a blessed thing this side of resurrection. Vessels on high shelves sit poised, ready to topple and shatter upon hard floors. Pride is burdensome and is known for preceding falls. Can it be so bad to be delivered of this?

Thank God for the comfort of mistakes. Mistakes remind us of our clayhood and drive us toward Christ. When we finally quit chasing perfection and accept these vessels of clay, we will become happier. When we forget about ourselves, peace will ensue. The happy acceptance of imperfection is the beginning of easy breathing. Because, really, how can you be peaceful and flogging yourself simultaneously? You can't. That's why no one in a religion is truly happy. People in religions act happy because they're expected to, but they're only one step away from disappointing their deity and suffering his wrath. How happy can they truly be?

Pages 34-36

In the Bible, God is always getting humans into scrapes so that He can get them out of the scrapes and show His power. You say, "No, Martin. God isn't getting the humans into the scrapes. The humans are getting themselves into the scrapes." Well, that theory works fine until you consider accounts such as the hardening of Pharaoh's heart. And we're going to do that shortly. But first I want to show you how God delights in making things humanly impossible before He sets to work.

Remember the story of the blind man Christ healed? What is the first thing the Lord does? He spits on the ground, makes mud, and then smears the mud on the man's eyes. Then He tells the man to go wash in the Pool of Siloam. The guy comes back reading *The Jerusalem Post*. Just when you think God is crazy with this mud business, you start to wonder, *Maybe God is making a point. Maybe mud on top of blindness is God's way of compounding a problem.*

Consider 1 Kings, chapter 18, when Elijah challenged the prophets of the false god Baal to a contest, to see which God was real. Elijah and the prophets of Baal would each set up an altar. Each would pray to their God to send fire down to their respective altars. The God who sent fire down would be the true God. The prophets of Baal went first.

According to verse 26 of that chapter, the prophets of Baal "called on the name of Baal from morning until noon, saying, 'O Baal, answer us.' But there was no voice and no one answered. And they leaped about the altar which they made."

No Baal. It was Elijah's turn.

Notice the curious thing Elijah does to his altar. I'm quoting from verses 33-35. Elijah said, "'Fill four pitchers with water and pour it on the burnt offering and on the wood.' And he said, 'Do it a second time,' and they did it a second time. And he said, 'Do it a third time,' and they did it a third time. And the water flowed around the altar, and he also filled the trench with water.'"

With the dousing of the altar, Elijah, through the spirit of God, was setting up a field of "impossibility" on which God would demonstrate His power.

Is God making some things impossible for you? Is God dousing your life with water? And when you seem about to recover, is He dousing you a second time? Then a third time? Is there running water in the trenches of your life? Are you getting ready to put on your swimsuit, sit down, and stare at your insurmountable trials? Good. The sooner you do that, the better off you'll be. God has purposely dampened your life with impossibilities, in order to bring you to the end of yourself. The result is that you will be in a relaxed position (flat on your back, for instance, or on your face) to hear and see His new plan for your life. ■

Martin,

I heard you on a radio show in Chattanooga, TN about a year ago. You debated a Baptist minister. The host sent me one of your books: *Flawed by Design*. I had been a Baptist from a young age until about twenty. Then there were too many questions that didn't add up, so I became mostly an atheist.

When I read your book, I nearly went deaf because of all the clicking sounds. Those were the sounds of all those things in the Bible that didn't add up, clicking into place. I credit your book as the means God used to allow faith in Him to return to me. I now realize that Christ died on the cross for all our sins and His grace is sufficient to save us. —*John P.*

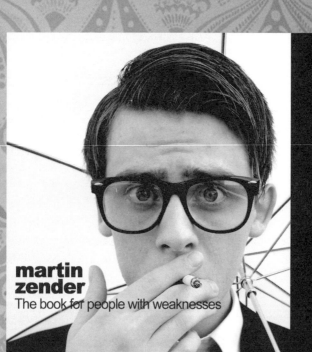

martin zender
The book for people with weaknesses

**HOW TO BE FREE FROM SIN
WHILE SMOKING A CIGARETTE**

EXCERPT

HOW TO BE FREE FROM SIN WHILE SMOKING A CIGARETTE

Pages 11-13

I don't smoke, but I sometimes wish I did. I have other questionable habits I won't burden you with. But I can picture myself holding a cigarette, or letting it hang cockeyed out of my mouth like Humphrey Bogart used to do. Whenever I talked—mumbled, I mean—the cigarette would bounce up and down. Then I'd squint and say something devilish to Lauren Bacall.

In this fantasy of mine, I know smoking is bad for me. I know it's wrong. I know I'm sinning, even while I'm doing it. But I do it anyway because it's cool, because life has been unfair to me, because Bacall has great legs, and because if I don't do *something*, I'll lose my mind. It's the worse kind of sin: knowing it's bad, but doing it anyway.

Preachers today lower their voices when speaking of such badness. They'll talk all sing-songy about stock sins like anger, jealousy, and pride. I call these stock sins because they're a dime a dozen. I'm not saying they're not bad, but I find myself doing them without even thinking. The sins I'm talking about—the sins that make the preachers furrow their eyebrows and talk like Vincent Price—are the ones where the wretched sinner says, "Yes, this would be a sin, all right," then does it anyway.

According to the clergy, there's no refuge for this. It's not like it's an accidental sin. It's not like it's a one-time deal. It's more like, "We're sorry, Lord, for what we did today. And we're sorry, too, that we're probably going to do it again tomorrow. And the day after that. And the day after that." The only comfort from the pulpit for this kind of badness is the remote possibility of a Sno-cone stand in hell. So no matter what your particular weakness is—

Well, hold on a minute. It just occurred to me that maybe you don't have a weakness. This is something I had not considered until now, and it changes everything. This project is shot if most of my readers don't have a weakness. If you don't have a weakness, how can I let you waste your time reading a book about weaknesses and how to deal with them? If you don't have a weakness, then please accept my apology, return this book to your bookseller, and use the money you saved to send a real sinner to Bible camp.

This book is written only for those who know what they're supposed to do but sometimes don't do it. It's written for those who think that their own particular weakness keeps God from completely liking them. It's written for those who just can't shake a bad habit. This book is written for the wretched souls who totter between their passion life and their desire for God, not realizing that in order to have a desire for God they must also be dogged by at least one nagging passion that keeps them humble and needing Him. It was wrong of me to assume the worst of you. So forgive me, please, and have a blessed day.

For those who do have a weakness—or two—welcome to paragraph seven. It appears that we've lost a few of the religious folks. At least now we can speak honestly among ourselves.

We're believers. Or we're seekers. Some of us love Jesus Christ already; others aren't sure if we want to or not. In either case, there are bad things we all do occasionally (or continually, perhaps) that dismantle our happiness in front of God. They've got a term for this dismantling that is so weighty and terrible it deserves its own paragraph.

The term is guilt.

Is it possible to be free from sin, even while sinning? Is it possible to be free from sin and the guilt associated with it, even while narrowing your eyes at Bacall and leaning toward her match?

I know what religion has told you. Religion has told you that freedom from sin means you don't sin anymore. But is this God's thought? If this is God's thought, then no one today can be free from sin—at least none of the honest people who made it past paragraph six. But I generally find that God's thoughts and the thoughts of orthodox religion are two different things. I'm happy to report it's also the case here.

This book is written and dedicated to all the poor sinners in the world who can't stop sinning, but who love or want to love the Lord, Jesus Christ. Here's the good news: *You have already been freed from sin.*

Thanks for hanging on. God's Word is about to deliver you from discouragement, condemnation and guilt, without asking you to change a thing you're doing. On second thought, you may have to change one thing. If you've been beating yourself over the head trying not to sin, you're going to have to quit that. Stop assaulting your head.

You still here? Great. That last paragraph wasn't a joke. I would never joke about something as serious as sin. How could I possibly tell you to quit pummeling yourself over it? Because this monumental effort—and the repeated failures and inevitable guilt trips that follow—is ruining your opinion of yourself, taking away your peace, and robbing you of the affection due Christ. You're working so hard trying to *impress* Him that you're not paying enough attention *to* Him.

"But if I let down my guard for even a second," you say, "I'll sin like a crazy person."

Hold on. That's what religion has told you, and I just suggested that religion is usually wrong. It's wrong here, for sure. Religion supposes that by keeping a moral watchdog chained to your flesh, you'll stop sinning. You've probably already disproved this theory with many a botched New Year's resolution. The Pharisees disproved it 2,000 years ago.

Pages 19-20

Before his trial, Scripture describes Job as "flawless and upright." This is verse 1 of chapter 1. But then Job loses his family, his wealth, and his health. Now listen to him in chapter 10, verse 1: "My soul is disgusted with my life; let me give free rein to myself and my concern; let me speak in the bitterness of my soul." Ah, there's the real Job, the mess of a man that was seething beneath that skin all along. But before he could understand his weakness, Job had to be broken. Can you imagine your Christian brother or sister even thinking Job's "blasphemous" words? No one would invite the real Job to the Wednesday prayer meeting, at least not without asking him to comb his hair and keep his scabby mouth shut.

George Bernard Shaw was a genius. It was he who said: "Virtue is insufficient temptation." Many times, those who appear virtuous have not been sufficiently tempted. Their virtue is Hollywood-wall virtue, propped up with half a dozen two-by-fours and a New Year's resolution. It's self-control untested. The world can spot phony Christian virtue ten miles away. Christians can't see it because they are too busy admiring themselves in the mirror.

Real human virtue is being broken by trial and lying like a pile of lumber in the wake of a hurricane. That's when the good stuff starts; it's when God goes to work. Real human virtue is helplessness before God. Helplessness before God is the beginning of a true spirituality that stands strong when the wind blows. Well, it has no place to go but up.

Romans 5:8—"Yet God is commending this love of His to us, seeing that, while we are still sinners, Christ died for our sakes."

God went out of His way here to say, in effect, "I did not justify you in your Sunday clothes. I did not justify you while you were loving your neighbor as yourself, or praying to Me in the quietness of your room. Instead, I justified you while you were yelling at your children, running up your credit card, stuffing yourself with donuts—and worse. I did this for you on your worst day, not your best. I did it this way so that you could thank Me the rest of your life instead of wasting your time trying to figure out how to downplay your faults and impress Me."

What did you say, God? Our robes were rustling.

When God justifies us this way, we're finished before we start. Since He did His best for us at our worst, what can we do now to improve the relationship? Act better? But He already did His best for us while we were acting our worst. What can we do now to blow our relationship with Him? Sin? But He already maxed out on His love for us while we were sinning like crazy people. ■

Dear Martin,
I stumbled across your book at the library while researching other faiths and was instantly intrigued. As I read, I could literally feel the guilt falling off of me. I swear I feel 10 pounds lighter each day because I no longer pack my sins around with me. I feel the love of God more clearly now than ever. The reality of God's grace is beautiful. The pure logic of it is so obvious now, but was so hidden before. Thanks be to Him, and to you for voicing it. The only regret I have is that it took so long for me to truly experience the power of the cross.   —Susan R.

EXCERPT
THE FIRST IDIOT IN HEAVEN

From the back cover

While on Earth, Jesus said some difficult things. He told the rich to give away all their money, and the joyful to become mourners. If you wanted to inherit the Earth, you had to be meek. If your eye offended you, no problem—as long as you plucked it out. A friend of mine said, "Can I start following Jesus on Monday? I'd like to enjoy the weekend."

Obviously, the words and commandments of Jesus are pure, perfect, holy—and meant for Israelites. Jesus Himself said, "I was not sent except to the lost sheep of the house of Israel" (Matthew 15:24).

Is it possible we have been struggling along someone else's path? What if the words in red were never meant to be our marching orders?

Several months after leaving Earth, the Jewish Messiah appeared as a very non-Jewish light to a self-righteous idiot en route to Damascus to kill Christians.

Up next? Not only a startling new destiny for believers (heaven instead of Earth) but a new message of pure grace for all humanity.

This is that story.

Pages 15-16

You want to live like Jesus, you really do. You're sincere as can be, but it's an uphill climb. You love people and you love God, so maybe today will be the day you can finally imitate His Son. Maybe today you can finally be meek, turn the other cheek, and rejoice while getting mud thrown in your face.

Think how good it would feel to be pure—to have no sin and no guilt. Think how good it would feel to wake up calm each morning, love everyone during the day, and rest your head at night with a prayer for your enemies.

If only.

And yet it never quite works out that way. In the darkness of your bed each night, you know who you are. Jesus was Jesus, but you are you. When you curl up beneath the covers, you face the terrible truth: It has been another day of failure and frustration.

If only there were a gospel in the Bible for common, ordinary human beings. Or even mediocre people. It seems the gospel of Jesus that tells us to live like Jesus sets the bar just a little too, um, *high*.

I know all about it. I was raised Catholic. The nuns told me all I had to do was be meek and mild like Jesus (plus do everything else like Jesus) and I would go to heaven. It seemed like a tall order for someone with cartoons on his underpants. What did I know? All I wanted was to play football and eat candy.

Pages 18-19

Why do we have such a difficult time shaping up and producing fruit worthy of repentance? Maybe better to ask: Why do we instinctively know we *can't* do these things? Why do we give up *trying* to do them? Is it because we are lazy? Ungodly? Satanic? Because we think we deserve nothing more than to be crushed beneath God's fist? Or could it be that, deep down, we think God doesn't really expect us to weep and wail, repent, and be practically perfect in every way? But if He doesn't expect all that, what do we do with all the Bible verses saying He does expect it? Could it be there are *other* Bible verses that say *different* things?

Are you bold enough to entertain a new thought? What if we, who are not Israelites, have a different gospel—*in the Bible*—than the one meant for Israel? What if this other gospel even has a different name? What if it has a different set of requirements (and a different outlook on run-of-the-mill people or hapless nincompoops) than the gospel given to Israel? And—think of this—what if this gospel promises an enormously better destiny than the one promised to Jewish believers?

Were faithful Israelites ever promised heaven? Not once. Jesus Himself said, "The meek shall inherit the *Earth*" (Matthew 5:5). Wouldn't Jesus have known what He was talking about? Israelites never dreamed of getting lifted from Terra Firma. Why would they? Jesus never spoke to them of such a thing. And neither did their prophets. Faithful Israelites were promised that they would rule and reign over the other nations of Earth. This was the promise God made to Abraham.

Back to my question. What if this different gospel I have been referring to (the easier one; the kinder and gentler one; the one that caters to those of us who are not-so-perfect) *does* take people to heaven? Wouldn't that be mind-boggling? It would mean that the nuns at my school were all wrong. Imitating the walk of Jesus would not have gotten me to heaven—as she insisted it would—but would, instead, have kept me on Earth to rule the other nations. What *would* get me to heaven would be giving up trying to be like Jesus and embracing a gospel for regular folks—assuming such a gospel actually exists.

Wouldn't that be something God would do? Bless the socks off average, ordinary people? Doesn't it align with everything we know about His penchant to stun loser-types (fishermen, prostitutes, tax-collectors) with draughts of favor? So God gives reformed sinners (obedient Israelites) what He promised them—namely, Earth—but then later announces a *different* gospel that seats unworthy people (those who haven't a prayer of being like His Son) at His right hand in the highest regions of heaven.

Would this be a gospel you'd like to learn about? ■

Just finished my first reading of *The First Idiot in Heaven*. I had never heard of Martin Zender, or this message. I am astounded! I had begun to think something was wrong with me. That perhaps God wasn't interested in me. That I was simply not invited to be in His family. I could not figure out why I could not understand either the bible or what my church taught. God knows how desperately I've wanted to. It is as though scales have been lifted from my eyes! I HAVE PRAYED FOR THAT SO MANY TIMES. I can't wait to learn more and my heart is crying out to be a herald. Thank you, Lord God ,and thanks to Mr Zender!   —*Gordon S.*

MORE READER COMMENTS:
The First Idiot in Heaven

"Martin, What can I say? Wow! Thank-you. I just ordered a bunch of *First Idiots* to give to friends who love wisdom, humor, and revelation. Everything was laid out just right, and succinct. Paul himself would be amazed. Thank you for not giving up your calling."   —Kathy K.

"Hi Martin. I'm having a book while reading your beer! It's very, very good, but you've gotta know: They're gonna kill you for this one Zender ;) Love your work! Grace and peace from Norway!"   —Erik S.

"I have been a Zender fan since his first book took the scum off of my eyes 15 years ago and gave me great peace. This book is a continuation of that peace. I can only say: Thanks, Martin. Were it not for you and your books, I would be truly confused and lost in a man made religion.   —Bud M.

"Wow! Just finished *The First Idiot in Heaven*, and I think it is your best book yet. That's a big deal, since the others were so excellent. I hated to see the pages count down to 0."   —James F.

"A must-read. The Evangel entrusted to Paul is so beautiful when contrasted with the Circumcision gospel. This book clearly differenciates the two. My prayer is that Father opens many hearts to *The First Idiot in Heaven*. This is a classic Zender book to be read and reread." —Max P.

"Best Zender book ever! (That's saying a lot.) I love the delivery, the humor, the wisdom. From the moment I picked up this book, I only put it down to go to work. Instant classic."   —Darron H.

"Written with such clarity. Liberating, and nearly effortless to understand. No more anguish, guilt, shame. Martin, THANK YOU."
—Susan L.

"This is the methodical, Scripturally-backed work I've always longed for. My deepest questions are answered. An articulate illustration of the difference between the writings of Paul and the rest of the Bible. Clearly, Martin's most powerful book to date.   —Jana L.

All my life, since I was about 6, I knew God was not in a box, knew there was freedom. In February of 2009, I heard you and Dan on the radio for the first time. My kids and their friends have always known me to be someone who stuck with God's word and Holy Spirit, rather than with some slick preacher or formal church. I literally cried when I heard you guys for the first time! I wonder if you really realize how dramatic this can be for folks who feel like they have just come home? Thank you for being bold!

—*C.V., San Francisco*

The
MARTINZENDER
DANSHERIDAN
Show

WBRI
indianapolis

 www.martinzender.com

My husband, 2 grown sons and I have been listening to your daily messages for a couple of years now. You are refreshingly different. I've been on a search for truth for about 10 years. We listened to a variety of Internet messages but settled on yours because it's dependable, funny, and best of all is NOT like regular church teaching. The gift you've been given is clarity. It's not a commonly possessed gift! —*M.R., Atlanta*

Dear Martin, Please keep the Clanging Gong News coming! We are a couple of families living in eastern Iowa, and have been getting together for fellowship for a few years now. Yo are a breath of fresh air to us! I have been known to read sections of your newsletter out loud, with tears in my eyes. God put you in our lives at exactly the right time. Keep doing what you do!   —*A. B., Cedar Rapids*

Volume 1, Issue 21

July 4, 2009

Martin Zender's Clanging Gong News

"If I know all mysteries and all knowledge, but have no love, I am a clanging gong" --1 Cor. 13:1-2

Two out of three isn't bad.

God is a man. Not.

From last week's mailbag.

Dear Martin: So what you're saying is that all the misery and pain in the world, God is responsible for. That seems very twisted and punitive to me, like we have this capricious God playing a cosmic chess game. I can't say I like serving a God like that.

—B.T. Memphis, TN

Dear B.T.

If you're serving a God like that, then you're serving a God of your own invention. God is neither twisted, punitive, nor capricious. And he does not play games.

I'm sure this chess player is a nice man. But he isn't God.

Concerning misery and pain, it's not about what I'm saying, but about what Ephesians 1:11 is saying: "God operates all in accord with the counsel of His will." So yes, "all" would certainly include all misery and pain. Your job is to believe Ephesians 1:11 and then trust God. Instead, you're believing Ephesians 1:11, but then assuming that God is a man; man is twisted, punitive, capricious, and a game player. Yikes, B.T. Are you sure you want to put the Deity into that same category?

The vital point of last week's edition was: temporary evil is essential to eternal bliss. The vital point here is: God is not a man.

Yours because of grace,

Martin

Behind the scenes at the creation of Satan

Before He could demonstrate His power, love, and salvation, God needed an enemy to wrestle against. Since enemies were once non-existent, God had to create His own. God did not enjoy creating an adversary. In fact, He hated it; it pained His heart. And yet, for the ultimate sake of His creatures, He had to do it. So He did.

I pray that, by the time you finish this article, you will see God's heart in the creation of evil. I want you to see how hard it was for Him (in the short term) to provide for your eternal happiness and security.

You believe Him, but you hesitate to embrace Him.

cussed with you before, there can be no such thing as eternal happiness and eternal security without the very real and painful struggle against adversity. God did this for you, not to you. Still, He wrestled with it.

Some of you are writing me—especially on the heels of last week's edition—telling me how

you balk against believing in a God who created evil (Isaiah 45:7), and made the Adversary the way he is (Jn. 8:44; 1 Jn. 3:8). Those of you strong enough to accept this scriptural fact tend to hold such a God at arm's length. It's as if you do not fully trust Him. You can *believe* in a God Who creates evil, but you hesitate to embrace that One. Deep down, you fear Him. Today, I want you to change your heart and mind about God.

How can you continue fearing your Father? How can you continue fearing the One Who demonstrated His love for you by sending His only Son to die for your sake? How can you

(Continued on page 2)

CGN PRESENTS: **THE CRAZY FAMILY**

"God has nothing whatsoever to do with this toothache!"

"I'm *glad* Satan has a realm of untouchable sovereignty."

"Serving an out-of-control Deity is the awesomest!"

"A loving God in total control of this world would be, like, a *nightmare!*"

"Um, will someone please get me the heck out of here?"

"OMG!" —*Cynthia F.*

www.youtube.com/zendermeister

www.martinzender.com